SOFT FURNISHINGS
for the
BEDROOM

By the same author

The Batsford Book of Lampshades
The Batsford Book of Curtains and Window Treatments
The Batsford Book of Soft Furnishings
The Batsford Book of Home Furnishings

SOFT FURNISHINGS
· *for the* ·
BEDROOM

ANGELA FISHBURN

B T BATSFORD LTD   LONDON

ACKNOWLEDGEMENTS

The author would like to thank the following for the loan of colour photographs: Dorma: front jacket, 1 and 3; Stencil Decor: back jacket and 8; Pallu and Lake: 2 and 6; Charles Hammond: 4, 5 and 7, and also the following for the loan of black and white photographs: Curtain Net Advisory Bureau: 1, 2, 7 and 9; Dorma: 3; Stencil Decor: 4 and 5; Rufflette: 6, 8 and 10.

Thanks also to Nicola Thomas for the line drawings.

ISBN 0 7134 5455 5

Printed in Great Britain by
Richard Clay (Chichester) Ltd
Chichester, West Sussex
for the publishers B.T. Batsford Ltd
4 Fitzhardinge Street, London W1H 0AH

Contents

•

CONTENTS

Introduction 7

ONE
Stitches and techniques 8

TWO
Tools and equipment 21

THREE
Fabrics and style 24

FOUR
Curtains and blinds 30

FIVE
Cushions and lampshades 37

SIX
Country-style bedroom 44
Unlined curtains 44
Frilled piped cushions 47
Throw-over bedspread 50
Bed valance 53
Pleated firm lampshade 57
Circular tablecloth 59
Fabric-covered photograph frames 61
Herb cushions and lavender/pot pourri sachets 63
Covered coat hangers 65
Waste paper bins/cotton wool holders 67

SEVEN

Plain and tailored bedroom   70

Lined curtains with pencil pleating   70
Pelmets   73
Roller blind plus stencilling   77
Box cushions for bedhead   80
Tailored bedcover   82
Bolster cushions and buttoned cushions   84
Duvet covers   85
Fitted and plain sheets   87
Pillowcases   89
Cone lampshade   91

EIGHT

Classic country house bedroom   95

Interlined curtains with pinch pleated heading   95
Curtain tie-backs   98
Gathered valance   103
Bed drapes and canopies   105
Loose cover for a headboard   107
Dressing table cover   108
Classic style lampshade   110
Roman blinds   114
Swags and tails   117

NINE

En suite bathroom   121

Festoon blind   121
Loose cover for ottoman/stool/trunk   124
Squab cushion with ties   126
Austrian blind   128
Tissue box covers   130
Bath cushion   132
Shower curtain   132
Towel trims   134
Bath and shower cap   134

Suppliers and useful addresses   136
Glossary   138
Bibliography   139
Index   141

Introduction

•

INTRODUCTION

Making soft furnishings for the home has become a very popular pastime over the last few years, with many people having a keen desire to learn both the basic techniques and the more advanced skills necessary to enjoy this most fascinating and rewarding area of home making.

In this book I have concentrated on sewing for the bedroom (although all the techniques can be applied to other rooms too). Our bedrooms can be havens where we can escape and relax; they reflect our most personal ideas and idiosyncrasies, so it is perhaps here that we can combine flair with originality.

I hope you will enjoy using the ideas that I have suggested and that the techniques and skills described will help you to create a thoroughly pleasing and professional result. The bedroom is surely one of the most important rooms in the home.

ONE

Stitches and techniques

•

Here are some of the stitches and seams most frequently used when creating soft furnishings and other accessories for the home.

STITCHES

Tacking (basting)

Tacking or basting is temporary stitching used to hold two or more thicknesses together. There are two types of basting: (a) long equal stitches of about 1.3 cm (½ in) with equal space between and (b) two stitches of 1.3 cm (½ in) and one stitch 2.5 cm (1 in) long. The latter is particularly useful when tacking up curtains and other large articles, as it is quick to work. Stitch from right to left. Start and finish both types of basting with backstitch to secure (*Figs 1 and 2*).

Backstitch

Used where a strong seam is required and where it is not easy to use the machine. Stitch from right to left taking the needle back the length of the stitch behind and bringing it through the length of the stitch in front.

Keep the stitching even and approximately 6 mm (¼ in) in length (*Fig 3*).

Prick stitch is very similar but worked on the right side of the fabric. A very small backstitch is worked and it is sometimes used when inserting zips because it gives an unobstrusive line of stitching.

Running stitch

Worked on the right or wrong side of the fabric from right to left, and used when gathering by hand. Keep the stitches even, with equal spaces in between (*Fig 4*).

Overcasting

Used to neaten a raw edge to prevent fraying, if a machine with a swing needle (zig zag stitch) is not available. Work from left to right, bringing the needle through at an acute angle and taking the thread over the raw edge (*Fig 5*).

Herringbone stitch

This is worked from left to right, usually over a raw edge. It is used for making hems on heavier fabrics where extra strength is necessary and for securing interlining to the

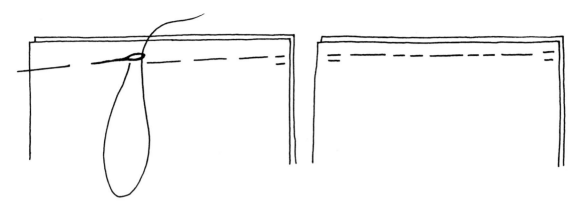

1 TACKING, OR BASTING, USING LONG EQUAL STITCHES

2 TACKING USING ONE LONG AND TWO SHORT STITCHES

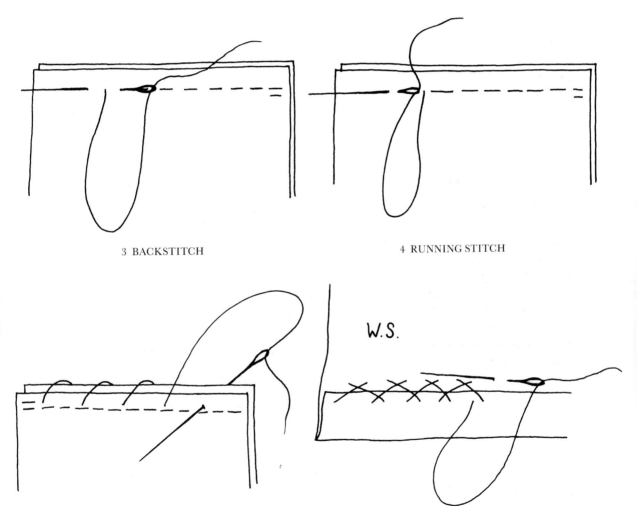

3 BACKSTITCH

4 RUNNING STITCH

5 NEATENING A RAW EDGE WITH OVERCASTING

6 HERRINGBONE STITCH

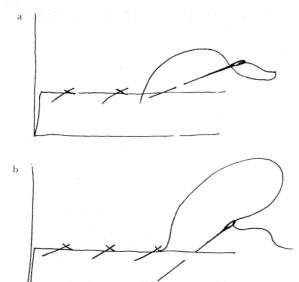

a

b

curtain fabric when making interlined curtains. As this is a decorative stitch it can also be used for appliqué. Keep the needle pointing to the left and the thread on the right-hand side of the stitch. Pick up a thread of the folded fabric and then a thread of the single layer of fabric. Keep the stitches as close as possible to the raw edge (*Fig 6*).

Serge stitch

Used when turning down a single fold hem on the raw edges of a curtain before the lining is applied. Work from left to right picking up a thread from the single thickness of fabric and then inserting the needle into the folded edge. The two stitches should be made in one movement and be approximately 1.3 (½ in) in length. The stitches should not show on the right side of the fabric (*Fig 7*).

Hemming

Work from right to left on the wrong side of the fabric. Insert the needle just under the fold, taking a thread of fabric, and then insert the needle into the hem. Do not pull the thread tightly (*Fig 8*).

Lockstitch

This is a long loose stitch, approximately 10-15 cm (4-6 in) in length, used to 'lock' or secure curtain linings and interlinings in position. It is worked from left to right down the length of the curtain using a long length of thread. Keep the stitches very loose so that no pulling occurs when the curtains are hanging (*Fig 9*).

Slipstitch

Used for joining folded edges together invisibly as on a mitred corner, also when stitching curtain linings in position. Pick up

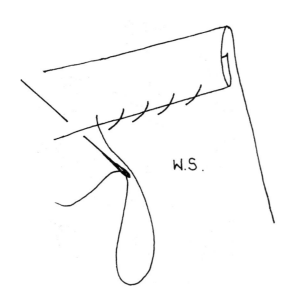

W.S.

8 HEMMING

10

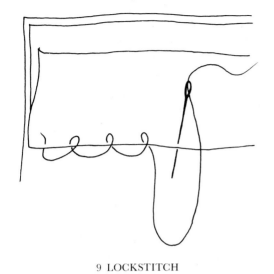

9 LOCKSTITCH

a thread from one fold and slide the needle through the fold for 6 mm (¼ in). Put the needle into the other fold and carefully draw up the thread. Do not pull tightly or you will get puckering (*Fig 10*).

Outside tacking (slip tacking)

Used for matching patterns accurately and worked on the right side of the fabric so that the pattern is easily visible. Fold in the edge of one piece of fabric onto its wrong side and place onto the right side of the piece of fabric to be matched. Place the pins into position horizontally, carefully matching the pattern. Slip tack, taking a stitch on the fold of the one side and slipping the needle down through the fold on the other. Stitch the seam in the exact position of the tacking line so that the pattern matches accurately (*Fig 11*).

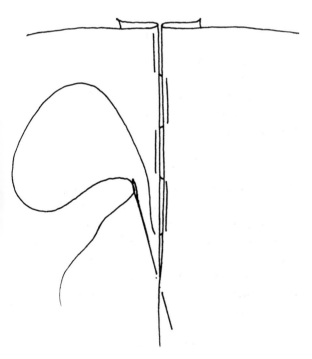

10 SLIPSTITCH

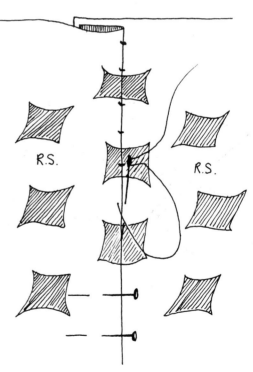

11 MATCHING PATTERN REPEATS USING OUTSIDE TACKING

SEAMS

Plain seam

This is the most usual seam used in soft furnishings and can be worked by machine or by hand using a backstitch. Place the fabric with raw edges together, right sides facing, and tack 1.3 cm (½ in) from the edge. Stitch the seam, remove the tacking stitches and press open. Neaten the raw edges where necessary with a row of zig zag stitching, or overcast by hand. Alternatively, the seam can be neatened with seam binding. When machining a curtain seam or other long seam always stitch down the length of the seam from the top to the bottom. Make sure that the nap (pile) runs in the same direction on each side of the seam – point to watch particularly when sewing velvet or corduroy. When machining on fine fabrics, PVC or leather, use strips of tissue paper between the fabric and the machine presser foot to make stitching easier. Do not tack or use pins on PVC or leather; it would spoil the fabric. Instead, use sticky tape to hold the materials together whilst stitching (*Fig 12*).

Lapped seam

Use this seam on fabrics that tend to stretch easily, such as bump or domette. Lap one raw edge of the fabric over the other and tack. Machine seam with two rows of zig zag stitching (*Fig 13*).

French seam

This seam is used when widths of lightweight fabric are being joined together and raw edges need to be enclosed. It is only suitable for fabrics that are not thick and bulky. It is a strong and hardwearing seam, useful when making pillow cases, duvet covers and unlined curtains.

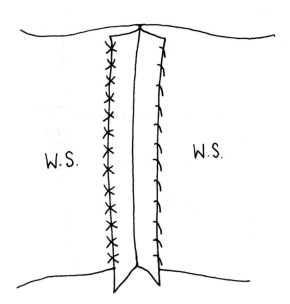

12 NEATENING A PLAIN SEAM WITH A ZIG ZAG MACHINE STITCH, OR OVERCASTING IT BY HAND

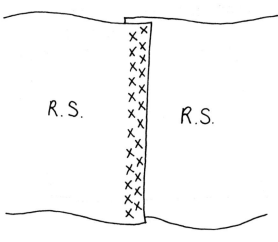

13 LAPPED SEAM USED FOR JOINING INTERLININGS

Place the two pieces of fabric together, wrong sides facing. Tack and stitch approximately 6 mm (¼ in) to 1.3 cm (½ in) from the edges. Trim the seam and turn to the wrong side. With right sides together tack and machine to enclose the raw edges (*Fig 14*).

Flat fell seam

This is a useful seam when joining widths of fabric where a strong enclosed seam is required but the stitching shows on the right side of the fabric. Place the wrong sides of the fabric together and have the raw edges even. Tack and machine 1.3 (½ in) from the edge. Press seam open. Trim one side of the seam to 6 mm (¼ in) and turn in the raw edge of the other side 3 mm (⅛ in). Fold this over the trimmed edge and machine close to the fold (*Fig 15*).

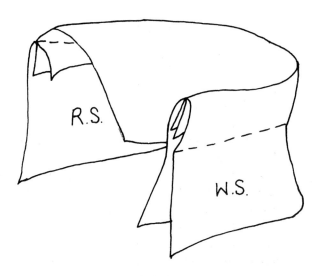

14 FRENCH SEAM WITH RAW EDGES ENCLOSED

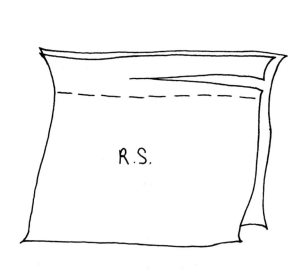

15a TRIMMING THE SEAM ALLOWANCE TO MAKE A FLAT FELL SEAM

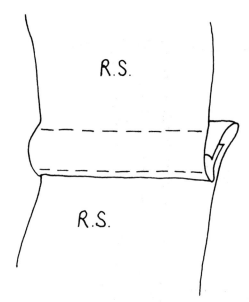

15b FLAT FELL SEAM

13

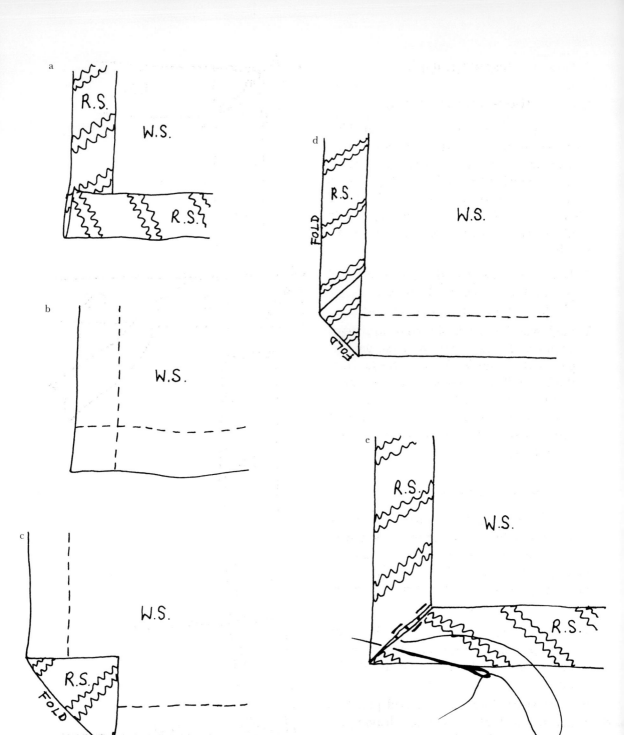

16 MITRED CORNER

TECHNIQUES

Mitred corners (*Fig 16*)

A mitre is a fold used on hems when making curtains, pelmets, bedspreads and other items where a smooth well-shaped corner is required which does not look bulky. Folded mitres are used on the hems of lined and interlined curtains and can only be properly made when the two hems are the same width.

1 Fold in the two hems the same width and press (*a*). Open out the hems so that they are flat and the fold marks show (*b*).

2 Fold over the corner of the fabric at right angles to the fold marks to make the first part of the mitre (*c*). Press. If the fabric is thick or bulky, cut away some of the mitre to give a smoother finish. Fold the hems again at the side and lower edge to complete the mitre (*d*). Slipstitch the folds together (*e*).

Decorative borders (*Fig 17*)

These are attractive when made in contrasting fabrics and colours and applied to the edges of curtains and to cushions, blinds, bedcovers etc. It is a useful way of decorating plain or textured fabrics. Make them 5-10 cm (2-4 in) wide.

1 Cut strips of fabric equal in width and overlap them at right angles, making a line of tailor tacks from A to B (*a*). Cut tacks.

2 Place right sides together and pin, tack and machine along this line, leaving the seam open 1.3 cm (½ in) at each end so that the edges of the border can be folded in (*b and c*). Trim the seam to 1.3 cm (½ in) and press open.

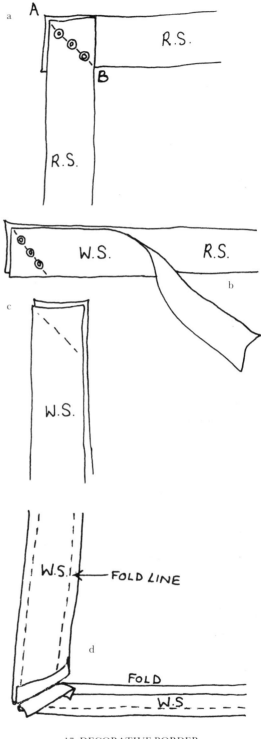

17 DECORATIVE BORDER

3 Turn under and press 1.3 cm (½ in) along the two raw edges of the border and apply to the curtain, valance etc. (*d*).

Edges

Frills

A gathered or pleated frill can be used to make a pretty edge for curtains, cushions, pelmets, tie backs etc. Vary the width of the frill to suit the item being decorated. Narrow frills are usually made from double fabric.

Gathered frill

To make a 7.5 cm (3 in) frill, cut a piece of fabric one and a half to two times the length of the edge to be frilled, joining fabric pieces if necessary. When making a continuous frill (for a cushion, tie-back or pillowcase), join the short edges of the strip together, fold and press in half lengthwise and make two rows of gathering stitches 6 mm (¼ in) from the raw edges. When making a long frill, e.g. bed valance, divide the strip into sections and gather each section separately. This prevents the threads breaking and enables the gathers to be evenly distributed. With right sides together, pin and tack the frill to the fabric being trimmed and arrange the gathers evenly. Allow a little more fullness at any corners. Tack and machine into position.

Pleated frill

Cut out and prepare the strips of fabric as for the gathered frill, but allow three times the length if making knife or box pleats without a space between. Pin into pleats, measuring accurately. Tack and press. Make two rows of machine stitching, 6 mm (¼ in) from the raw edges, to hold the pleats into position. Apply to the fabric as for the gathered frill.

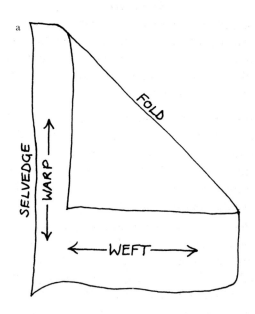

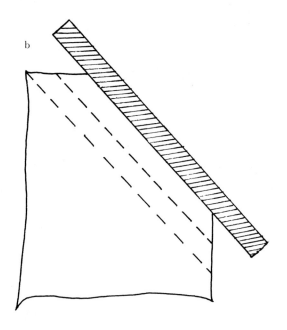

18 CUTTING FABRIC ON THE CROSS

Bound edge

A bound edge is made from strips of fabric cut on the bias or cross grain of the fabric. It should be cut three times the required finished width; Usually a strip 3.8-5 cm (1½-2 in) is wide enough.

1 Prepare strips of fabric using the method described here on cutting fabric on the cross. If large quantities are required use the quick method of cutting on p. 19. Remember to join the strips on the straight of the grain (*Fig 19*).

2 Place the edge of the crossway strip to the right side of the edge to be bound. Tack and machine 1.3 cm (½ in) from the raw edges. Turn the strip to the wrong side and fold in 1.3 cm (½ in). Pin and tack so that the fold comes onto the line of machine stitching. Hem by hand so that the stitches are worked on the machine line.

Cutting fabric on the cross (*Fig 18*)

1 Fold the material diagonally so that the selvedge thread lies across the crossway thread, i.e. the warp across the weft (*a*). Press. Cut along the fold. The fabric is then on the true bias or cross grain.

2 Make a ruler in stiff card 3.8 cm (1½ in) wide to use as a guide. This ensures that all the strips are cut exactly the same size. A wider ruler, 5 cm (2 in) wide, could be used when covering thicker cords.

3 Place the edge of the ruler to the cut edge of the fabric and mark with a sharp piece of tailor's chalk, making parallel lines the same width (*b*). Cut along the lines and continue until sufficient strips have been made.

Joining bias strips (*Fig 19*)

All joins made on bias or crossway strips should be made on the straight grain of the fabric. Place two strips together with right sides facing making sure the ends are cut on the grain. Pin and stitch the seam, making sure that the strips form an angle (*a*). Press the seam open and trim away the corners (*b*).

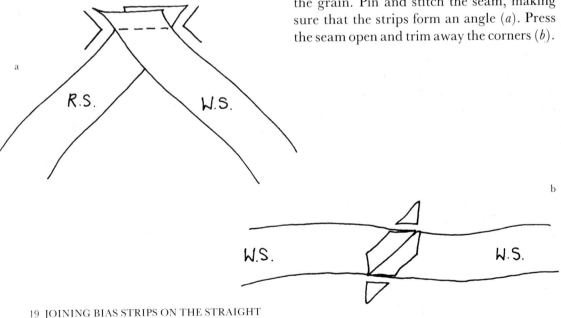

19 JOINING BIAS STRIPS ON THE STRAIGHT GRAIN OF THE FABRIC

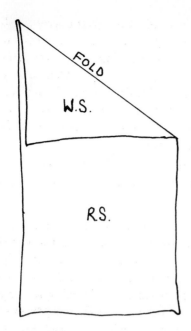

a

FOLD

W.S.

R.S.

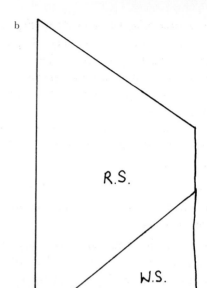

b

R.S.

W.S.

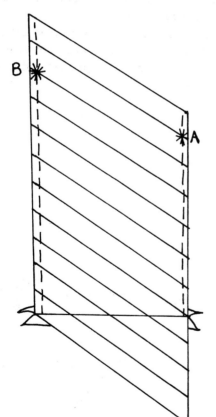

c

B

A

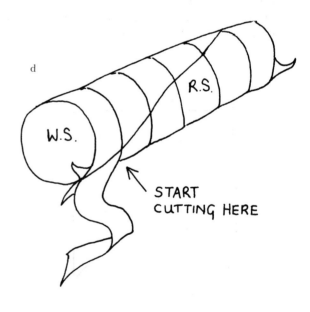

d

R.S.

W.S.

START CUTTING HERE

20 QUICK METHOD OF MAKING BIAS STRIPS

Quick method of making bias strips (Fig 20)
When several metres of bias strips are required for making cushions, loose covers etc., it is useful to be able to prepare them without having to join each strip separately. This simple method can save much time. A quarter of a metre (or ¼ yd) of fabric makes 5 metres (5 yd) of bias binding 3.8 cm (1½ in) wide.

1 Take a strip of fabric 23 cm (9 in) wide. The length of the strip should be at least twice the width.

2 Fold over the top right-hand corner to obtain the direct cross (*a*). Cut off this corner and join to the lower edge with a 6 mm (¼ in) seam (*b*). By adding this piece no fabric is wasted.

3 With a ruler 3.8 cm (1½ in) wide, mark lines on the right side of the fabric with a sharp piece of tailor's chalk, parallel to the top edge. Mark a 6 mm (¼ in) seam allowance down each side and mark the first and second lines A and B (*c*).

4 Take a pin through the wrong side of the fabric at point A and take this across to point B, pinning very accurately with right sides together. Continue pinning along the seam. Tack and stitch the seam, checking first that the lines match up exactly, in order to make a tube. Press the seam open.

5 Turn to the right side and start cutting round the tube at the projecting strip at the top edge (*d*).

If larger pieces of fabric are available, the top right-hand corner and the bottom left-hand corner can be cut off and set aside. This produces the same shaped piece of fabric but has the advantage of having fewer joins in the tube. Remember, though, that the length of the strip of fabric must be at least twice the width, or more.

Square pieces of fabric can be used in a similar way by cutting in half diagonally and joining as in Fig 21, placing right sides together.

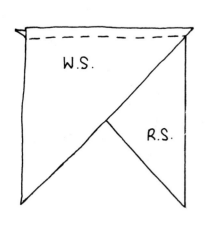

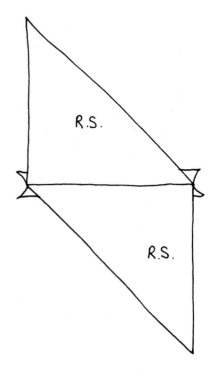

21 USING SQUARE PIECES OF FABRIC IN A
SIMILAR WAY

19

Covering piping cord

Use strips of fabric cut on the bias or cross grain of the material to cover cotton or synthetic piping cord. This can be sewn into the seams of cushions, loose covers, bedcovers etc. As well as strengthening seams it also makes a smart decorative edge for blinds, pelmets, curtain tie-backs etc. and is also used for neatening raw edges. It has many uses when making soft furnishings for the home.

Piping cord can be obtained in several different thicknesses. Choose from fine, medium or coarse depending on the item being decorated. Cotton cord should be carefully shrunk before use; otherwise, when washed or dry-cleaned it will shrink and the strips of fabric covering it will pucker. Most cord is sold as shrink resistant, but if no guarantee is given, shrink it by boiling it for five minutes in a saucepan of water, drying it carefully before use.

Fabric cut on the cross has more 'give' and is much more flexible than that cut on the straight of the grain. This means that it is easier to apply to a curved edge, as it moulds well and sets properly. To be really successful it should always be cut on the true bias or cross of the fabric.

The strips used for making a decorative piped edge show up best in fabrics that contrast well with the item being decorated. However, try to match weights and textures of the fabrics carefully for the best results. Loosely woven fabric is not suitable, as it wears out quickly.

Joining piping cord

Join piping cord by cutting it. Butt the two ends together and bind with thread to hold them securely, making sure that they do not overlap; this would make a bulky finish.

TWO

Tools and equipment

•

Make sure that tools and equipment are of good quality and in efficient working order, and use them only for the purpose for which they were intended. Replenish the workbox regularly with new pins and needles and look after them carefully. Bent needles result in poor workmanship and rusty pins will mark fabrics.

When scissors need sharpening it is best to return them to the manufacturer or have them professionally ground.

Pins

Choose good-quality steel dressmaking pins, as these will not pin-mark fabrics. Never use rusty pins. Glass-headed pins are often used for making lampshades but they are very sharp and extra care is needed when using them. Invest in a new packet of pins regularly and keep them carefully in the box or tin provided for that purpose. Do not leave pins in fabric longer than necessary for they will mark the fabric if left for long periods.

If a finger is pricked and blood accidentally stains the fabric, remove it by chewing a piece of tacking thread then rub this onto the bloodstain and it will remove the stain without leaving a water mark.

Needles

Make sure needles are sharp and free from rust. Include a variety of different sized needles for various types of fabrics and threads.

Sharps and Betweens 7-9   For general use.

Crewel/Embroidery These are the same length as Sharps but the longer eye makes it easier to thread embroidery and thicker threads.

Bodkins Blunt, thick needles which are useful for threading elastic, cords etc. through casings.

Threads

It is important to use the correct thread. Match the thread colour to the fabric but have it one tone darker. Use synthetic threads with synthetic fabrics. These are strong and can damage natural fibres, but cotton thread used on synthetic fabric would shrink more than the synthetic fabric and cause it to pucker. Use cotton (50) or multi-purpose cotton-coated polyester threads with light medium-weight natural fibres and No.40 for heavier materials. Use silk or No. 60 cotton for silk or finer fabrics, and tacking cotton for basting.

21

Scissors

A sharp pair of cutting-out shears with specially bent handles makes the cutting out of fabric for curtains and blinds easier. A smaller pair of scissors 12.5-14 cm (5-5½ in) is useful for cutting threads etc. Choose the best quality possible.

Measures

Rules

A wooden metre/yardstick is invaluable for measuring curtains accurately. An inexpensive one can be obtained from most wallpaper shops. Alternatively, use a metal rule. A large set square can be useful when cutting out lengths of fabric. A rigid rule is essential when measuring curtains, blinds and windows.

Tape measure

Choose a fibre-glass or linen tape with a stiffened end. These are the most reliable as they will not stretch easily.

Thimble

Choose a metal one to protect the middle finger. It is almost essential to get used to wearing a thimble for it makes things much easier when sewing coarse fabrics such as roller blind and firm lampshade fabric.

Weight

A weight is very useful when making curtains and blinds. It is used to prevent the fabric from slipping from the table, and a simple one can be made easily from a brick or an old iron. Cover the brick with pieces of old blanket or wadding and then cover with some strong fabric. Make a handle from upholstery webbing so that the weight is easy to move. Its padded top can be used as a pin cushion.

Tailor's chalk

This is extremely useful for marking fabric when cutting out curtains, cushions and blinds. It is obtainable in several colours as well as white, though white is the easiest to remove. Do not use pencils or pens on furnishing fabrics.

Seam ripper

Sometimes called a *quick unpick*, this is a useful ripping tool for unpicking seams and stitches quickly.

Upholstery pins and skewers

Useful for holding fabric in position when making chair covers etc.

Ironing board and iron

A wide board is the most useful and a steam or heavy iron the most suitable for home furnishings. Man-made fibres sometimes leave marks on the base of the iron. Clean the base regularly using a non-abrasive cleaning cream, making sure first that the iron is switched off and cold. Keep the iron readily available for pressing each stage of the work. Use a clean white cloth for pressing; it prevents scorch and shine marks on the fabric. Check the fabric manufacturer's instructions for ironing; also check the temperature of the iron, and test a small piece before making up.

Cutting out surface

Use a large table for cutting out. A wallpaper pasting table provides an ideal surface and can also be used for pressing if covered with a thick blanket. This type of table is a good investment as it is relatively inexpensive and can be folded up and stored easily. Do not attempt to make curtains on the floor: it isn't good for the back and it makes the fabric dirty.

Sewing machine

A sewing machine is essential for making soft furnishings, as many long seams often have to be worked. A sewing machine should last a lifetime, so time and careful thought should be given to its selection. Choose a lightweight, versatile machine with a free arm and one with a zig zag facility for neatening seams and edges. An electric machine leaves the hands free to control the fabric.

Make sure that it is strong enough to take several thicknesses of fabric and that it has a presser foot attachment that enables stitching to be worked as close as possible to the piping cord when making cushions and other piped items. This particular foot is of greater importance than others which provide the means of sewing a wide range of embroidery stitches but which will probably be used less often.

Make sure you know how the machine operates, taking advantage of any after-sales tuition that may be offered. Learn to thread up the machine quickly, and practise changing the needles and presser feet to suit the fabric and thread being used. Study the instruction manual carefully. Clean and oil the machine regularly and have it professionally serviced from time to time. Keep the machine covered when not in use and do not leave it in a cold damp room or in direct heat. Never leave it with the electric plug connected, as this could burn out the motor.

Notebook

Keep a notebook for making cutting-out plans and writing down measurements and fabric requirements.

THREE

Fabrics and style

•

CHOICE OF FABRICS

When furnishing the home it is important to remember that it is not only curtains and carpets that are necessary to achieve a good visual effect but also all the smaller accessories such as cushions, lampshades, padded hangers etc. These smaller items all add up to the very special place that we call home, where we should be comfortable and happy. A successful decorative scheme is one that always gives us pleasure, confidence and satisfaction.

Fabrics fall into two categories – natural and man-made. Natural fibres are based on raw materials from animal and vegetable sources; man-made fibres are those manufactured by chemically treating raw materials such as minerals and vegetables. Great developments are taking place in the manufacture of man-made fibres and progress is constantly being made, with new processes and techniques improving the properties of the fabrics. It is frequently very difficult to distinguish them from the natural fibres which they imitate. Sometimes they are even more practical, needing less care and maintenance than their 'natural' counterparts.

When choosing and buying fabrics for the bedroom there are many points to remember.

1 Choose and buy the best quality fabric that you can afford; this may not necessarily be the most expensive but it should be the one that offers the best value for money. In the bedroom it is possible to use less durable fabrics, as they will not be subject to quite the same wear and tear as in living rooms and halls.

2 Dress fabrics are not made to withstand constant exposure to light and atmosphere so are not usually suitable for curtains and covers; but they can be used successfully for lampshades, cushions and other small home accessories. Dress fabrics will not wear as long as furnishing fabrics. They are also narrower and more seams are necessary; extra care must therefore be taken when checking fabric requirements.

3 Read the manufacturer's label carefully to see whether the fabric is shrink-resistant, fade-resistant, crease-resistant, etc., and note any instructions for

washing and dry-cleaning. It is worth visiting fabric showrooms and shops that specialize in furnishing fabrics to see the fabrics displayed. The staff here are trained to help and advise and to answer questions about the composition, care and suitability of the fabrics chosen.

4 When selecting a fabric for loose covers choose one that will resist dirt well and will not crease. It is important to choose a closely woven fabric that is hardwearing and washable. Poor quality fabrics wear quickly and soon need replacing. Choose textured fabrics, random match patterns or small prints, as these are much easier to handle when making up.

5 Curtain fabric should drape well and be fade resistant. Extend its life by protecting it from strong sunlight and frost with a suitable lining. Unlined curtains or blinds will not have this protection.

Ask to see the material draped in order to check its draping qualities and to see its pattern and colour. If possible ask for pattern samples so that they can be considered at home both in daylight and in artificial light and in the setting for which the fabric is required. Some shops are happy to provide large pattern samples which are returnable when a choice has been made. If this is not possible, buy a small quantity of the fabric which can later be used for making a cushion or a lampshade.

6 Choose a well-known manufacturer when selecting patterned fabrics, and make sure that the pattern is printed correctly. If the pattern is not woven into the fabric, check that the design is printed correctly on the grain. This is essential when choosing fabrics for curtains, as the lower hem should be turned up with the grain for the curtains to hang well.

Small pattern repeats, or random match patterns are more economical than large patterns, where much wastage can occur. When making curtains an allowance of one pattern repeat to each length or 'drop' of curtain (or blind) should be made. Some patterns work better than others, but if in doubt check with the sales assistant.

7 Check fabric carefully for flaws. These should be marked on the selvedge with a coloured thread. It is important to check before cutting into the fabric since, quite naturally, some shops will not make allowances if the material has been cut.

8 Buy enough fabric to complete the project, and buy from one roll only. If necessary, place a special order. It is not always possible to obtain exact colour matches at a later date and dyes vary with each batch.

9 Check the 'finish' of the fabric, making sure that it has real body and not just a dressing that will disappear the first time the fabric is washed or dry-cleaned.

10 Consider some of the more unusual fabrics – denim, mattress ticking, calico. These are often a good choice when economy is necessary or when furnishing children's bedrooms. They give unusual and pleasing results and some are very hard-wearing.

CREATING A STYLE

Here are some ideas on the decorating scheme.

1 Consider the aspect of the room. North- and east-facing rooms require warm colour schemes to counteract the lack of sunshine and low intensity of light. Choose the warmer tones of red, oranges or yellows. In contrast, rooms with strong sunshine can take the cool fresh colours of blues and greens.

2 Collect samples of fabrics suitable for the main items of soft furnishing such as bed covers and curtains. Use complementary colours for the smaller accessories such as cushions and lampshades.

3 Distribute colours around the room so that the overall effect satisfies the eye. Too much pattern in one place can create an unbalanced effect. Experiment by placing furniture in different positions if possible, giving emphasis to a particular feature. If possible place chairs so as to take advantage of any sunlight.

4 Look at good design wherever possible and observe how pattern and shape are used. Much can be learned by studying the work of professional designers in their different fields, e.g. television, films, window displays, magazines, brochures etc. Be constantly aware of the 'design' that surrounds us. Visits to stately homes and historic houses can also be a great source of inspiration.

5 Keep a scrapbook and collect cuttings of ideas and schemes that have special appeal, but do not copy a room setting precisely – let it be an inspiration for the creation of your own ideas.

6 Light colours create spaciousness and make a room larger and lighter. To create an illusion of space avoid large patterns on fabrics and walls and keep them in proportion to the size of the room.

7 Dark colours have a warmer effect than light ones. Spots and stripes work well with patterned of plain fabrics.

8 Gathered valances and shaped pelmets give a room a traditional look, whilst frills and patchwork suggest country cottage charm.

9 Try to create an integrated colour scheme for the whole house or flat. This is not always possible but can probably be achieved gradually over a period of time. Colours can be linked by the choice of a basic floor colour. Pick out a colour in one room and work round it to create a pleasing scheme for the next, and so on, using variations in texture, colour and pattern. The eye will then not be confused with too many colours and the effect will be restful and harmonious.

10 Heavy interlined curtains and thermal linings are useful in bedrooms where noise and light are a problem. They effectively cut out light and sound and are also good insulators.

11 Furnishing on a budget is a challenge but there are many good decorative ideas that are inexpensive and simple to adapt to individual needs.

12 Take time when choosing fabrics and creating a decorative scheme. Do not be rushed into buying something you are not sure about. Never buy fabric in sales unless you have had a chance to consider it first and know that it is exactly what you want. Never be tempted to buy

without your samples and patterns in your hand – it is almost impossible to carry colour in the eye.

FABRICS FOR SOFT FURNISHINGS IN THE BEDROOM

Polyester/cotton sheeting

This fabric is made partly from natural cotton fibres and partly from man-made fibres. It therefore washes well, does not crease easily and needs little ironing. It comes in widths suitable for making into single and double sheets as well as duvet covers and pillow cases and is very versatile because it is made in co-ordinating plain colours and prints. It is useful for making matching bed valances, curtains and blinds, and can be used for covering small bedside tables.

Cotton lace

This is available in wide widths and can be used for making bedcovers, curtains and blinds. It is likely to shrink when washed, so generous allowances should be made for fullness and hems. Most lace is hand or machine washable and needs pressing with a cool iron.

Bump

A thick fluffy fabric made from cotton waste. It is usually 122 cm (48 in) wide and is used for interlining curtains and pelmets, and is a good insulator. It cannot be washed and must by dry-cleaned only.

Domette

This has the same uses as bump but is not quite so thick and fluffy. A raised interlining, similar to domette but made from man-made fibres, is now available and this also needs to be dry-cleaned and should not be washed.

Synthetic wadding

This is available in various widths, weights and thicknesses and has many uses. It is completely washable and non-absorbent and is therefore a useful filling for cushions, duvets, quilts and pillows.

Pelmet buckram

This is golden brown in colour and made from coarse canvas impregnated with glue. It is sold by the metre in narrow widths (usually 45.5 cm [18 in]) and is used for making curtain tie-backs as well as pelmets.

Buckram

This is obtainable by the metre and varies in depth from 7.5 cm (3 in) to 15 cm (6 in). Used for stiffening hand-made curtain headings.

Downproof cambric

A firm, closely woven cotton fabric which is specially waxed on one side to prevent the down working through the fabric. The waxed side should be placed next to the filling in order to be effective. Use this for making duvets that are to be filled with down of any kind, and also for making cushions and pillows with down or feather fillings.

Unbleached calico

This is a strong cotton fabric which is comparatively inexpensive and very hard wearing. It has many uses, e.g. for the base section of bed valances where strength is required. As it tends to shrink it is best washed before use.

Pillow ticking

This black and white striped fabric can make attractive hard-wearing blinds, but it is mainly for making pillows. It is usually 140 cm (54 in) wide and is also available in plain white.

Holland

This is the traditional firm fabric used for making roller blinds. Many colours are available in wide widths, so joining is often unnecessary. It repels dirt and dust well and does not fray at the edges.

Velvet

Velvet and velveteen can be made from silk, cotton or synthetics and varies in quality with the fibres used, the closeness of the pile and the background onto which the pile is woven. Take care that the pile is placed always in the same direction when making curtains – this is usually *downwards* in soft furnishings, *upwards* in upholstery. This prevents dust being caught in the pile and gives a pleasing effect when the curtains are draped. Pin and tack velvets carefully before machining seams, for when the piles are placed on top of one another the fabric tends to slip out of position.

Chintz

Usually a 100 per cent cotton fabric which has a shiny or 'glazed' finish, this is particularly attractive and repels dirt and dust well. Use it for making curtains, cushions and blinds. In order to retain its full glaze this fabric should be dry-cleaned.

Linen union

Its high linen content makes this a hard-wearing durable fabric which is ideal for loose covers of all types. It is available in a very wide range of patterns and a good range of plain colours.

Gingham

This is available in weights suitable for curtains and blinds, and with its fresh crisp look is particularly suitable for children's rooms and bathrooms.

Lining sateen

A closely woven cotton fabric normally used for lining curtains and blinds. It is available in a wide range of plain colours. Choose the best quality available as it tends to shrink when first washed or when dry cleaned.

CARE AND MAINTENANCE

1 Take care when selecting fabrics for soft furnishings that they will both suit the decorative scheme and be thoroughly practical in use. Consider also their position – will they be in a rural setting or in an urban location where they will need more frequent washing or cleaning? Children's bedrooms usually need hard-wearing fabrics that wash or clean well. Interlined curtains and insulated linings are useful in bedrooms, but need to be dry-cleaned and cannot be washed.

2 Textured and slub fabrics attract the dust more easily than those with a smooth or shiny surface; this may mean that they need cleaning more often. Plain fabrics show the dirt more quickly than most patterned ones. As dirt makes the fibres of the fabric wear out more quickly, try to keep soft furnishings as clean as possible by brushing or vacuuming them regularly with a special attachment. This helps to lengthen their life.

Make yourself familiar with the fibre content, and follow manufacturers' instructions on the care label. Check washing and drying instructions given on washing powder packets.

3 Most man-made fabrics wash and dry quickly, retaining their shape well. They do not shrink or stretch and usually have a good resistance to sunlight, which makes them an ideal choice for curtains and blinds. Sheers and nets made from man-made fibres such as nylon should be washed before they get dirty.

4 Do not pre-wash fabrics when making curtains, blinds etc. as this often removes special finishes, such as glaze. It sometimes changes the appearance of the fabric too, and makes it soil more quickly. The exception is when using calico (e.g. for a bed valance). This tends to shrink and is best washed before making up.

5 Remove spots and stains from fabrics as quickly as possible using a weak detergent solution or a dry cleaning aerosol. Check that the fabric is colour fast and if possible experiment first on a small section that does not show.

6 Take special care when pressing velvet and use a velvet board if possible. Use a steam iron and press on the wrong side, making sure that the pile is not crushed.

7 If washing loose covers, iron the frill whilst still very damp. Stretch the cover on to the chair and finish ironing where necessary. In a centrally heated room this is usually unnecessary as the cover will dry naturally within a few hours.

8 Unlined curtains made from fabric that washes well can be laundered, with care, but most lined curtains are best dry-cleaned. Keep them as dust free as possible by brushing or vacuuming them regularly (using the special attachment) and airing them on the washing line.

9 Their buckram foundation means that pelmets need special care and are best cleaned *in situ* professionally. However, they can be kept clean for many years by regular brushing and vacuuming.

10 Interlined curtains need particular care with cleaning and need specialist treatment as they are composed of three very different fabrics.

11 Lampshades can be kept looking fresh and clean by regular brushing with a soft brush. Most soft fabric lampshades wash well. Choose a good drying day and wash gently in warm water using a mild solution of liquid detergent. Rinse thoroughly and hang on the washing line to drip dry. Most firm or rigid shades cannot be washed because of their paper content, so keep these clean by regular brushing. Some can be sponged clean, but this depends on the materials used.

12 Fabric-covered photograph frames cannot be washed and should be brushed to keep them dust free.

13 If curtain tie-backs have been constructed using a buckram foundation they should be dry-cleaned. Those made using a non-woven interfacing can be washed with care.

14 Roller blinds made from special blind fabric repel dirt and dust well but cannot be washed. Sponge them clean using a gentle detergent solution.

15 Festoon and Roman blinds should be treated as curtains. Unlined ones may be laundered with care, but lined ones are best dry-cleaned. Keep them well brushed or vacuumed to prevent dust collecting in the folds and gathers.

FOUR

Curtains and blinds

•

CHOOSING A WINDOW STYLE

Well-planned window treatments can do much to furnish a room, as together with floor and wall coverings they often provide the largest expanse of colour and texture, and thus can set the mood of the room. Windows were originally designed to let in light, and as life through the ages became safer, windows became larger and lower and curtains began to play an important part in the development of interior design and furnishing in the English country house.

Curtains and blinds have two important functions – they provide privacy and comfort, and insulation against cold and noise. Insulation may not be important in a hot climate or where there is double glazing, but in cooler climates and noisy cities it is pleasing to have something to draw over the window. Fabric can either be hung to pull sideways – as in curtains – or hung to pull up – as in roller, Roman and festoon blinds.

Many different effects can be achieved by the use of the various tracks, poles and fittings now available, and by treating windows with elegant pelmets or frilly valances. These can be made to suit the style of the room. Illusions of height and width can be easily achieved if care is taken with the treatment of windows and doors.

Most people have at least one problem window to treat and one of the features of modern living is the siting of radiators underneath window areas. This is always a difficult problem to overcome. In order to avoid heat loss, curtains can be made to overlap the radiator by 5-7.5 cm (2-3 in). Alternatively, use roller or festoon blinds and have floor-length dress curtains held back with decorative ties at the sides of the windows.

Curved windows and archways may be treated by using a flexible track which can be rounded to the shape of the window. Cover the headings of the curtains with a valance and Austrian blind tape. As they cannot be drawn, tie-backs must be used to hold the curtains back. Flexible tracks are also useful round bay windows and when treating dressing tables and vanity units.

Floor-length curtains are elegant in some bedrooms, whilst short, frilly curtains create an informal country style pleasing in smaller bedrooms and bathrooms. If the view from a window is unattractive, use blinds made

30

1 A PAIR OF MIRROR-IMAGE ROLLER BLINDS
MADE FROM DIAGONAL-STRIPED NET

from sheer fabrics. This is an attractive way of treating bathroom and bedroom windows where privacy is essential. Roller blinds are economical to make and can have dress curtains at either side of the window. This softens their rather hard line. Rolling right up to the top of the window, they give the maximum amount of light.

A Roman blind is a flat piece of fabric that pulls upwards in folds and is fixed to a wooden batten at the top of the window. It is similar to a roller blind, but instead of the fabric being rolled onto a roller it is pleated up the window in wide folds. Special tape is attached to the back of the fabric and cords threaded through loops on the tape to enable the fabric to be pulled up.

Festoon blinds are a decorative way of dressing a window. They hang in festoons in permanently gathered panels and are attached to a batten or a track at the top of the window. They are drawn up by cords at the back of the blind. Their construction is similar to Roman blinds but they need more fabric as they are permanently gathered both across the width and down the length of the blind.

Austrian blinds are similar to festoon blinds but have no permanently gathered panels. They hang in swags across the width of the blind when it is pulled up, and are very suitable for use in bathrooms and bedrooms.

Kits are available for Roman, festoon and Austrian blinds which contain everything required for making a blind apart from the fabric, thread, track and batten. Not all patterned fabrics work well with the scalloped effect of festoon and Austrian blinds, so choose small designs or random match patterns for the best result.

TRACKS AND FITTINGS

There are many different tracks, rods, poles and fittings to choose from and new and improved ones are often introduced. Some manufacturers provide helpful booklets on the many fittings and accessories available. A careful reading of these will help you to make the right choice. Some tracks and rods are easier to fix than others, and some have combined hooks and runners. Other tracks and poles have a cording system, which means that the curtain fabric is not handled so much in use. Not all tracks are pleasing to the eye but some can be covered successfully with curtain fabric or wallpaper. A pelmet or valance is an attractive way to cover them. Some tracks are not designed to take the weight of heavy velvet or interlined curtains, so check that they are strong enough to take the weight of the curtains they are to support.

LININGS

As well as helping the curtains to drape well, a lining helps to protect it from sunlight, dust and frost. All these damage the fibres of the fabric and make it wear out more quickly.

Choose a good quality cotton lining sateen. A poor quality one is a false economy as it will wear out before the curtain. An aluminium-coated fabric is also available which is a good insulator and is useful in bedrooms where light could be a problem.

Detachable linings can be made for curtains, using a special curtain lining tape. These are easily removed for washing and can be changed from one pair of curtains to another. They do not hang or drape as well but are useful when curtains need to be washed or dry-cleaned frequently.

Check that the lining sateen is the same width as the curtain fabric chosen, otherwise separate calculations must be made when estimating fabric requirements.

INTERLININGS

The use of an interlining in addition to a lining shows off the fabric to the best advantage. It gives body to thinner fabrics such as silks and dupions and is a good insulator, keeping out both noise and light. Use bump or domette for interlining, but remember that as neither one is washable interlined curtains must be dry-cleaned. A flanelette sheet could be used as a less expensive alternative.

CURTAIN HEADING TAPES

There are many decorative heading tapes from which to choose and these are used when making valances and blinds as well as curtains. The style chosen will depend on the effect required. Choose the best quality tapes you can, and from a well-known manufacturer, as some products are unreliable and their cords break when gathered. Several manufacturers produce interesting booklets on the different tapes and accessories they make and some give helpful advice on their use and application.

The pleating or gathering produced by commercial tapes is usually achieved by pulling up cords in the tape, or alternatively by inserting special pleater hooks into the pockets at regular intervals. Hooks should be removed from curtains and valances when they need to be washed or dry-cleaned.

New transluscent tapes have been introduced to make the construction of festoon, Roman and Austrian blinds easier and quicker. These are unobstrusive and therefore can be used successfully with lightweight and sheer fabrics, including lace.

Gathered heading

Standard pocketed tape 2.5 cm (1 in) wide produces a simple gathered heading ideal for use under pelmets or valances where the heading does not show. It can also be used on simple lined and unlined curtains when only a narrow frill is required above the heading. For a crisp finish, a strip of stiffening such as a non-woven interfacing can be inserted into the fold at the top of the curtain before the tape is applied. Allow 1½-2 times the width of the track when estimating curtain fabric.

Pencil pleats

Pencil pleats are produced by drawing up cords on specially stiffened tape. Tape is approximately 7.5 cm (3 in) deep and made in cotton and man-made fibres to suit both heavy and lightweight curtain fabrics. It has two rows of suspension pockets so that it can be used on any type of track or pole. Allow 2¼-2½ times the width of the track when estimating curtain fabric.

Pinch pleats

Pinch pleats can be achieved using different types of tapes. For example, one sort of tape draws up sets of pleats along the curtain automatically, leaving a space between each set of pleats. Another type has small single pockets along its width and the curtain is reduced by the insertion of special long-pronged pleater hooks that fit into the pockets. It is important to work out the approximate width down to which the fabric will pleat. The following is an example, but it

2 SLUB NET CURTAINS WITH AN ATTRACTIVE
SHIRRED HEADING

is best to pleat up the tape before applying it in order to work out the formula for the individual curtain.

122 cm (48 in) wide fabric pleats down to:

single pleat	*double pleat*	*triple pleat*
66 cm (26 in)	61 cm (24 in)	58.5 cm (23 in)

Arrange the hooks so that there is a single pleat at each end of the curtain. The rest of the hooks should be spaced out evenly across the curtain. Use four-pronged hooks for making triple pleats, three-pronged ones for double pleats and two pronged hooks for single pleats. Allow 2-2½ times the width of the track when estimating fabric requirements.

Cartridge pleats

These large cylindrical pleats are created by the use of draw cords on the tape. They look best when filled with wadding or tissue paper as this holds them round and firm. Allow twice the measurement of the track when estimating fabrics.

Once curtains have been hung on to the track or pole they should be 'dressed'. To do this, set the curtains into even folds 'breaking' the fabric between each pleat or sets of pleats, forward from the track so that they are proud of the pleats. Smooth the fold evenly down the length of the curtain then put two or three soft ties round the curtain to train them. If possible leave the curtains for a few days to 'set' the heading or pleating.

MEASURING AND ESTIMATING

1 If possible choose and fix the tracks or poles into position before estimating the amount of fabric required for the curtains. The track or rod is usually fixed 5-10 cm (2-4 in) above the window frame and should extend 15-45 cm (6-18 in) at each side of the frame. A wide window will need more room at each side to accommodate the curtains when drawn back. Interlined curtains also take up more space at either side of the window.

2 Measure the width of the track and decide where the curtains are to finish. Remember that a pole is a decorative feature and the curtains should hang just below it. Use a wooden metre stick or rigid rule to obtain accurate measurements and make a plan on paper, marking in the appropriate measurements.

If the curtains are to hang to the sill they should finish 5-10 cm (2-4 in) below the sill (or actually *on* the sill in some cases, e.g. a window seat). If a radiator is placed underneath the window, the curtains can be made to overlap the radiator by 5-7.5 cm (2-3 in) to avoid unnecessary heat loss. If the curtains are to hang to the floor, make them to finish within 1.3 cm (½ in) of the floor covering. Avoid any in-between measurement as the curtains will look out of proportion to the window.

These two measurements determine the amount of fabric required:

> (*a*) The width of the track (not the window).
>
> (*b*) The finished length of the curtains, i.e. the 'drop' measured from the position from which the curtain will hang, to their lower edge. To these measurements add a turning allowance for hems and headings of 15-23 cm (6-9 in) inclusive.

3 If using patterned fabric allow an extra pattern repeat on each 'drop' of curtain

when cutting; e.g. when four widths of fabric are needed, allow three extra pattern repeats. All the curtains should finish at the same position of the pattern. Plan them so that the pattern starts at their lower edge – after making an allowance for the hem of 5-6 cm (2-2½ in).

4 Decide how many widths of fabric are required to give the curtains the necessary fullness. This depends on the weight and thickness of the fabric and its lining and the heading selected. Light, unlined curtains need more fullness than heavy interlined ones. Here is a useful guide.

    (a) Simple gathered headings require 1½ times the width of the track.

    (b) Pinch pleats require 2-2½ times the width of the track.

    (c) Pencil pleats and some of the other decorative headings require 2-2½ times the width of the track.

To obtain the required fullness it is often necessary to join widths and half widths together. Err on the generous side and work to the nearest half width. Join half widths so that they hang at the outer sides of the window.

5 Unless it varies greatly in width, allow the same amount of fabric for linings and interlinings as for the curtain fabric.

CUTTING FABRIC FOR CURTAINS AND BLINDS

1 Use a large square or rectangular table for cutting out so that the end of the table can be used to square up the fabric where necessary (a wallpaper pasting table is useful).

2 If possible draw a thread in order to get a straight line across the grain for cutting. It is not possible to draw threads on all fabrics, in which case square up the fabric with the table or use a large set square to obtain an accurate cutting line.

Using tailor's chalk, draw a line across the fabric width; this should be at right angles to the selvedge. Cut along the line. Cut plain fabric to the grain of the material, but if a patterned fabric is printed slightly off the grain cut to the line of the pattern and not the grain.

3 Cut out each length of curtain, taking care to match the patterns. Mark the lengths of fabric with tailor's chalk and rigid rule before cutting. Allow for pattern repeats and turnings and check these carefully before cutting. Mark the top edge of each length of curtain as it is cut off the roll. This is particularly important when using plain or textured fabrics, or velvets, and makes it easier too when cutting patterned fabrics that have no obvious up/down.

4 When using patterned fabric, cut off any wastage as the lengths are cut. If this is not done, confusion can arise when making up the curtains and matching the pattern repeats.

5 Selvedges should be cut off where possible or snipped, as these often make the seams pucker. On loosely woven fabrics and those that fray easily, snip at 5 cm (2 in) intervals down the length of the fabric. As some patterned fabrics seem to have little seam allowance it is advisable to check first that the seams can be matched successfully before the selvedge is cut off.

6 Work the side and lower hems of curtains first. Measure the curtains to the required finished length and apply the heading tape last.

FIVE

Cushions and lampshades

•

Cushions are both decorative and functional and can be made in all shapes and sizes and from almost any type of fabric. They provide impact and individuality and can be decorated with frills and lace, patchwork and quilting and all types of embroidery. Cushions are costly accessories to buy but they can be made inexpensively from remnants of fabrics and from small pieces left from other home sewing projects.

Cushions for the bedroom are very fashionable and there is no end to the number that can decorate the bed. Much can be achieved with a little imagination and ingenuity. Experiment with stencilling on fabric using paints that match or contrast with the decorative scheme. Stencils and fabric paints are readily available. Try quilting the outline, thus adding to its interest.

FILLINGS

A good foundation is essential for a successful cushion and the correct filling should be chosen according to its function. Buy a cushion pad made from one of the following fillings, or make one following the directions on p. 38.

Down

The fine soft underfeathers of birds are very light in weight. This is an expensive filling but is soft and resilient and holds its shape well, and is a good choice for cushions made from fine fabrics such as silk or satin. About ½ kg (1 lb) is needed to make a cushion approximately 51 x 51 cm (20 x 20 in). Use down-proof cambric for making the inner cover so that the down does not work through the fabric.

Feathers

These are much less expensive than pure down but are heavy when used on their own. they are often mixed with down to make cushions for chairs and sofas. Featherproof ticking or downproof cambric should be used for the inner cover. About 1 kg (2 lb) feathers is needed for a cushion 51 x 51 cm (20 x 20 in).

Kapok

This is lightweight and inexpensive but tends to go lumpy with wear and is therefore not very long lasting. Use calico or sheeting for the inner cover.

Synthetic wadding

This is made from man-made fibres, is inexpensive and non-absorbent. The filling is washable and sometimes allergy-free. To make a cushion fully washable both the inner and the outer covers should be made in washable fabrics.

Latex and plastic foam

Can be obtained in blocks of various shapes, sizes, thicknesses and qualities and can be cut with a very sharp knife. It keeps its shape well but should be covered with a calico or strong cotton inner cover to protect it as it is affected by light and heat and will crumble with wear.

Plastic foam chips

An inexpensive filling, but does not have the same smooth appearance as other fillings. It does not absorb moisture. Use calico or cotton sheeting for the inner cover.

BASIC CUSHION SHAPES

Cushions can be made in all shapes. Square cushions vary in size from 30.5 cm (12 in) upwards. Round cushions can be made to any size with or without a boxed edge and can be made to fit stools or chairs, with or without ties. Variations can be made by cutting out shapes in triangles, diamonds, hearts or shells. Make a paper pattern first before cutting out the material, remembering that the filling will take up some of the fabric. Cut the pattern slightly larger to allow for this.

Delicate fabrics lend themselves to decorative edges such as frills, and heavier furnishing fabrics can be piped with fabric in contrasting colours.

MAKING A CUSHION PAD

To make sure that the finished cushion has a plump appearance make the inner pad 1.3 cm (½ in) larger all round than the outer cushion cover. For a 38 cm (15 in) square cushion the finished inner pad should measure 40.5 cm (16 in). This applies only when making cushions with loose fillings such as feather and down. Inner covers for latex or plastic foam shapes must be made to the exact size as this filling is rigid and firm.

Cut two pieces of fabric the size required, allowing 1.3 cm (½ in) turnings for seams. Place the right sides together and machine round the four sides leaving an opening of approximately 20.5 cm (8 in) on one side. When sewing downproof cambric use a fine needle and two rows of machine stitching. To prevent the filling working through the holes made by the machine needle, wax along the stitching with a piece of beeswax. Clip at the corners and turn the cover to the right side and fill. Sew up the opening with oversewing stitches, and wax if necessary.

OPENINGS FOR CUSHION COVERS

All cushion covers need an opening but this does not necessarily need to be permanent. A neater finish can be obtained by slipstitching the opening together when the pad has been inserted, and this method can be used on all cushions that are purely decorative. However, if a cushion cover needs to be removed regularly for washing or cleaning it needs to have a more permanent opening, e.g. a touch and close fastening or a zip fastener.

Leave an opening large enough to enable the pad to be inserted easily, making it to come within 2.5 cm (1 in) of the two corners on one side. Position the opening so that it shows as little as possible when the cushion is finished, having it at the back of the cushion or at the bottom edge, where possible.

LAMPSHADES

Successful lighting plays an important part in the decoration of a room. Lampshades are functional as well as decorative and should be chosen with care to suit their setting and their purpose. They are comparatively inexpensive to make, particularly if recovering an existing frame, or when making them using fabric left over from other soft furnishing projects.

LAMPSHADE FABRICS

Choose fabrics for soft lampshades carefully. Fine fabrics such as silks and satins are particularly suitable, as are lightweight furnishing cottons and some dress fabrics. Make sure that enough light filters through the fabric and check that it will not melt if placed near a light bulb. Do not use fabrics that are flammable.

Thick, non-stretchy fabrics are not suitable; those that are flexible and have plenty of 'give' are the best choice as they mould easily to the shape of the frame without wrinkling. Do not use fabrics that fray or split easily, e.g. rayon and satin dress lining fabrics, as they will need to be stretched quite tightly onto the lampshade frame; they also pin-mark easily and do not wash well. Use silk shantung and wild silks, fine dress cottons, crêpe de Chine, ginghams, lace, lawn and broderie Anglaise for best results.

If possible, use crêpe-backed satin for lining soft lampshades. This stretches well and is easy to use, and because of its shiny surface it reflects the light well and gives body to lightweight cover fabrics.

Choose pale colours for lampshades that are to be used for reading, for example by the bedside or in a bedroom/study, where maximum light is necessary.

CLEANING

Most soft lampshades can be washed with care. Wash the shade in warm water using a mild detergent. Rinse thoroughly and hang on the washing line to drip-dry. Dry the shade as quickly as possible and put in an airing cupboard for 24 hours afterwards as this helps to tighten up the fabric on the frame. If a contrasting coloured trimming has been used check its colour fastness before washing the shade.

Do not wash firm lampshades but keep them clean by regular brushing.

MAKING A FIRM LAMPSHADE

Firm lampshades are quickly and easily made. Their uncluttered lines make them an ideal choice to complement the modern styles of today; they look well in traditional interiors too.

Choose prepared lampshade card which is available from craft shops and department stores. Alternatively, buy a special PVC lampshade material which has instant adhesion on one side. Cut to the size required and press fabric, marbled papers or wallpaper, to the sticky surface, peeling off the protective paper as you work.

White buckram is a stiff cloth with a coarse rough weave which gives an interesting texture. It is useful foundation for painting and stencilling in oils or watercolours and can also be used for appliqué decoration using favourite pictures, such as cars, boats etc. (particularly suitable for children's bedrooms). When ironing fabric onto buckram, wipe the smooth side with a damp sponge before pressing on the fabric with a hot iron. Cover the fabric with a damp cloth and press again. Allow to dry thoroughly. Lace and embroidery can be mounted in this way. Dried flowers and leaves should be applied with an adhesive after the foundation material has been stitched to the frame.

Pelmet buckram, which is golden brown in colour, has an interesting texture and can be used effectively if it suits the decorative scheme.

Pleated conical shades can be made quite simply using wallpaper or other substantial papers (see instructions on p. 91).

CHOOSING A BASE

There are many bases available both in department stores and specialist shops, and some are sold complete with shades. Sometimes these lend themselves to decoration with paints (stencilling) and appliqué, and a ready-made shade can become an individual masterpiece.

Look out for bases with simple designs without too much fussy detail (*Fig 22*). Make sure that it is firm and that it will not tip over easily. Candlesticks and old vases make effective bases for lampshades and old ones can be converted at specialist shops. Decanters and other narrow necked bottles are not usually of the right proportions to make sucessful bases.

Match the line of the shade to the base so that the two together balance well and present a pleasing design of good proportions. As a general guide the diameter of the lampshade should be approximately the height of the base, or the height of the lampshade two-thirds the height of the base.

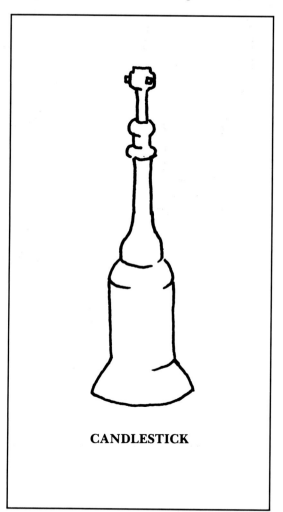

CANDLESTICK

22 CHOOSING A BASE

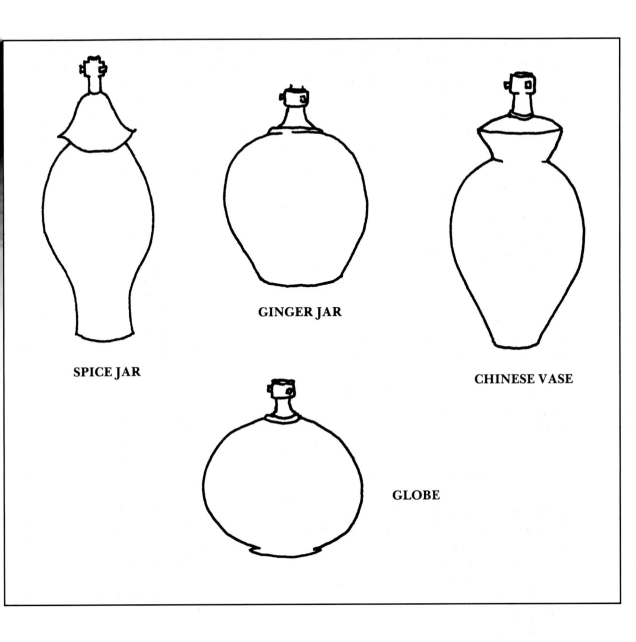

SPICE JAR

GINGER JAR

CHINESE VASE

GLOBE

FRAMES

Choose a firm sound frame that is free from rust or rough edges. This is the foundation onto which the fabric is stretched and sewn and it is rarely worth the effort involved unless a good frame is used. Bent frames result in distorted shades and the struts sometimes come away from the frame if the soldering is weak.

Choose a plastic-coated frame where possible, as these need little preparation and do not rust. When a frame has a tilting gimbal fitting, the plastic coating will cover the moving part and it is necessary to cut through the plastic with a sharp knife to enable it to work freely at both sides of the frame on the tilter fitting. If a plastic-coated frame is not available choose one that is made from a copper wire. This should be of a suitable gauge or thickness for the frame, enabling it to suppport the fabric firmly. File down any rough edges at the joints, other-wise they may push through the binding tape and fabric.

As long as they are not badly rusted or out of shape it is worth re-covering favourite old frames, particularly if they are of an unusual design. Take off the old binding tape and check for rust. File down or rub with fine sandpaper if necessary and paint the frame with a quick-drying enamel or gloss paint. Make sure that this is quite hard before attempting to bind with the tape.

Frames are made in many sizes for use with different types of fittings, so make sure that you choose the correct fitting for the light in question. Measurements are taken across the diameter of the base ring.

BINDING TAPE

Use 1.3 cm (½ in) wide lampshade tape or soft cotton tape to bind the lampshade frame. This is a poor quality unbleached/ bleached tape which is loosely woven. It is easily dyed with a cold water dye to match the colour of the lampshade lining, if necessary. This is useful when making a shade where the struts will show.

Taping the frame is an important process for it provides the firm foundation on which to pin and stitch the fabric. Make sure that it is firm, smooth and tight on all the struts and the rings. If it is loose the stitching will slip and the finished shade will be disappointing. When using plastic-coated frames it is only necessary to bind those struts where pinning and sewing will take place, but always tape the top and bottom rings.

TRIMMINGS

Trimmings are used on lampshades to cover stitches and sometimes seams, but they also decorate and complement the finished shade. Choose ones that relate well to both the base and the fabric, selecting silky braids and fringes for soft silky shades and using thicker more coarsely woven trimmings for cotton fabrics and firm lampshades. These more closely match the firmer texture of these materials.

There is a wide range of attractive commercially-made trimmings available but sometimes it is not possible to match colours exactly. If colours cannot be matched, use gold metallic braids or laces as these work well with many fabrics and can be used successfully with some hand-made trimmings, e.g. bias strips. Hand-made trimmings can be made using bobbin lace, crochet and tatting, as well as plaiting braids, wools, or rushes in various thicknesses. Machine embroidery can also be used to advantage to make scalloped and other decorative edges.

A trimming should always be sewn onto the lampshade where possible, unless a more even effect can be achieved by using an adhesive, i.e. when using narrow velvet ribbon, Russia braid or bias strip. Use a quick-drying invisible adhesive.

Estimate the amount of trimming required by measuring the circumference of the top and bottom rings. Add 5 cm (2 in) to each measurement, as the trimming should be eased onto the shade and turnings must be made. When applying trimmings make sure that the two joins at the top and bottom of the lampshade are made on the same side of the shade.

Fashions in trimmings change, so keep yourself aware of current trends by looking at good lighting departments to note any details of interest. Remember that a lamp-shade can be spoilt by the wrong choice of decoration.

SIX

Country-style bedroom

•

UNLINED CURTAINS WITH/WITHOUT FRILLS

Lightweight unlined curtains can be used successfully in bedrooms and bathrooms where privacy and ventilation are important. They are quick to make, wash and iron easily, and are simple to replace. Detachable linings can be used with these curtains when extra insulation and protection are required.

1 Estimate the amount of fabric required (*p. 35*) and cut out the fabric, matching the patterns carefully and using outside tacking (*Fig 11*). Join widths where necessary using a flat fell seam (*Fig 15*) and cut off the selvedges.

2 For a curtain without a frill, fold and tack 1.3 cm (½ in) double hems at the side edges. Machine stitch to ensure a firm edge. Fold up 5 cm (2 in) at the lower edge of the curtain to make a 2.5 cm (1 in) double hem. Tack and machine, taking care to make a neat finish on the right side of the curtain. Apply heading tape as required (see 6-8 below).

Single frill

1 For a curtain with a single frilled edge turn in the two side edges and the lower edge 1.3 cm (½ in) and press.

2 To make a 7.5 cm (3 in) wide frill, cut strips of fabric 10 cm (4 in) by the length needed, joining the strips if necessary, using French seams. To estimate the length needed to make the frill, measure round the curtain (omitting the top edge) and allow 1½-2 times this measurement. Make 6 mm (¼ in) double hems at the side and lower edges. Tack and machine stitch into position (*Fig 23*).

23 MAKING A FRILL WITH A CONTINUOUS STRIP OF FABRIC

3 In order to distribute the gathers evenly and to make it easier to handle, divide the strip into three or four equal sections (of not more than 91.5 cm [36 in] each). Work two rows of gathering stitches 1.3 cm (½ in) from the top edge of the strip.

4 Decide on the finished measurement of the curtains (remembering to take into account the frilled edge). Size up the curtains by measuring them from their lower edge to obtain the correct position for the heading tape. Measure along the curtains every 30.5 cm (12 in) using a rigid rule to obtain an accurate result. Fold and press down 2.5 cm (1 in) at the top edge of the curtain. This is where the heading tape will be applied.

5 At the sides and lower edges of the curtain open out the 1.3 cm (½ in) folded hems. Pin and tack the gathered frill to the fold line on the right side of the curtain fabric, stitching along the gathering line (*Fig 24*). Clip corners and distribute the gathers evenly, having a little extra fullness at the rounded corners so that the curtain hangs well. Trim the frill to 6 mm (¼ in) and fold over the 1.3 cm (½ in) hem allowance to make a bound edge (*Figs 25 and 26*). Tack the bound edge in position and press. Topstitch on the right side of the curtain. Alternatively, the bound edge can be slipstitched into position and the seam pressed towards the curtain fabric.

6 Measure the width of the curtain to obtain the amount of standard pocketed tape required and allow 2.5 cm (1 in) turnings at each end. Fold over the 2.5 cm (1 in) hem at the top of the curtain and tack the heading tape into position on the wrong side of the curtain. Turn in 1.3 cm (½ in) of tape at each end to neaten. For a curtain

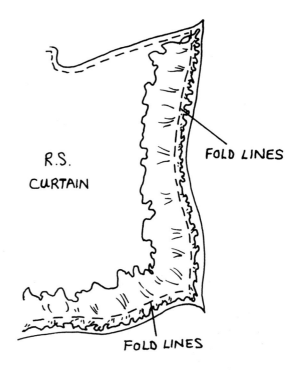

24 APPLYING THE FRILL TO THE RIGHT SIDE OF THE CURTAIN ALONG THE FOLD LINES

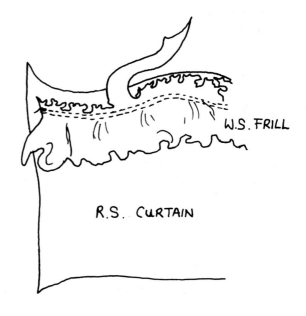

25 TRIMMING THE FRILL TO 6 MM (¼ IN)

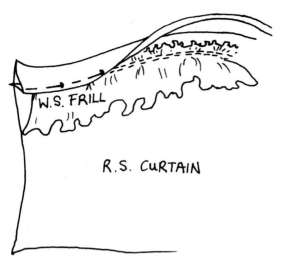

R.S. CURTAIN

W.S. FRILL

W.S. CURTAIN

26 TURNING OVER THE 1.3 CM (½ IN) HEM ALLOWANCE TO MAKE A BOUND EDGE

28 POSITIONING HEADING TAPE 2.5-3.8 CM (1-1½ IN) FROM THE FOLD LINE TO MAKE A FRILLED EDGE

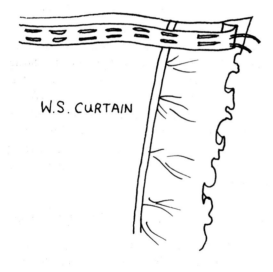

W.S. CURTAIN

27 APPLYING HEADING TAPE TO THE TOP EDGE OF THE CURTAIN AND THE FRILL

and position the tape 2.5-3.8 cm (1-1½ in) from the fold line (*Fig 28*).

7 Machine along the top and lower edges of the tape and along the two ends. When machine stitching tapes to curtains always stitch along the top edge of the tape first. Take out of the machine and return to beginning of stitch line, then make the second line of stitching at the lower edge of the tape in the same direction. This prevents the tape from puckering.

8 Insert curtain hooks into the heading tape every 7.5-10 cm (3-4 in) and draw up the cords on the outside edge of the curtain, distributing the gathers evenly. Do not cut off the ends of the cord but tie them neatly into a large bow or use a special cord tidy. These can be released easily when the curtains need to be washed or dry-cleaned.

that is to be positioned under a valance or a pelmet, stitch the tape into position 6 mm (¼ in) from the top edge (*Fig 27*).

To make a small frill at the top of the curtain, fold over 5 cm (2 in) at the top edge instead of 2.5 cm (1 in) (see 4 above)

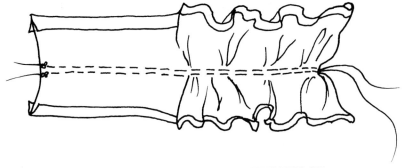

29 WORKING THE GATHERING STITCHES ON
THE TRIMMED DOUBLE FRILL

Double frill

1 For a curtain with a double frill make up
the curtain as above and make a 10 cm
(4 in) double frill by cutting strips of
fabric on the straight grain. Join these
with French seams where necessary to
obtain the required length. Trim the raw
edges of the long sides with bias binding
(matching or contrasting) or neaten the
edges by folding in 3 mm (⅛ in) double
hems. Machine stitch into position.

2 Fold the strip of fabric in half lengthwise
and divide into equal sections for
gathering. Work the gathering stitches
6 mm (¼ in) on either side of the fold line
using matching thread (*Fig 29*). Pin and
tack the centre of the frill to the hems of
the curtains along the stitching line and
machine into position. Carefully remove
the gathering stitches.

3 Complete the heading as for the single
frilled curtain.

FRILLED CUSHIONS

Frilled cushions are very pretty and as a
decoration on a bed they make bedrooms
look luxurious and relaxing. Choose fabrics
that match or contrast well with other
projects, but remember that lightweight
furnishing fabrics and some dress fabrics
work best for this type of cushion. Heavier
ones would be too bulky to gather well and
are therefore not suitable for this frilly style.
Make a double frill 5-7.5 cm (2-3 in) wide
(finished measurement).

Square and round cushions can also be
made plain with a piped edge in contrasting
or co-ordinating fabrics. Choose those that
are similar in weight and texture. Where
cushions are to be used for seating, or where
they will have heavy wear, remember to use
suitably hard-wearing fabrics such as strong
furnishing cottons, velvets, corduroys or
linen union.

Square frilled cushion with piped edge

1 Measure the cushion pad (see p. 38) and
cut out two pieces of fabric to the size
required plus 1.3 cm (½ in) turnings on
all sides. If the fabric frays easily or is
loosely woven allow 1.9 cm (¾ in) and
neaten the edges with a zig zag machine
stitch if possible before making up.

2 Prepare enough bias strip (3.8 cm [1½ in]
wide) to go round the four sides of the
cushion, plus a little extra for the join. Use
the quick method described on p. 19.

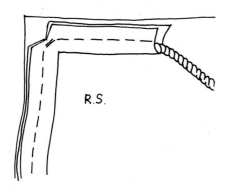

30 CLIPPING THE BIAS STRIP AT THE CORNERS OF THE CUSHION

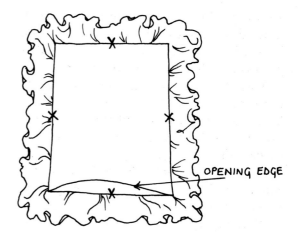

OPENING EDGE

31 DIVIDING THE CUSHION INTO FOUR EQUAL SECTIONS, AND LEAVING AN OPENING

3 Pin and tack the bias strip and the piping cord to the right side of the front section of the cover, beginning in the centre of one side. Tack close to the piping cord, using matching thread, and clip the corners (*Fig 30*) to enable them to be turned neatly. The bias strips can be joined as shown in Fig 19.

4 To make a double frill 6.4 cm (2½ in) wide, cut a strip of fabric 15 cm (6 in) wide on the straight grain. The length of the strip must be 1½-2 times the measurement round the four sides of the cushion pad. Join the short edges of the strip with a 1.3 cm (½ in) flat seam and press open. Fold the fabric in half lengthwise. In order to distribute the gathers evenly, divide the strip into four equal sections and work two rows of gathering stitch 6 mm-1.3 cm (¼-½ in) from the raw edges.

5 Divide the front of the cushion into four equal sections and mark these points *Fig 31*. Pin the frill to the front section, placing it over the piping cord. Distribute the gathers evenly round the cushion, taking care to have a little more fullness at each corner so that the frill sets well. Tack and machine into position.

6 Pin and tack the back section of the cover to the front section with right sides together. Mark an opening approximately 2.5 cm (1 in) from each end of one side of the cushion cover (the opening should be at the lower edge of the pattern, if there is one) and leave this unstitched (*Fig 31*). Machine into position using a zipper foot to enable the stitching to be positioned as closely as possible to the piping cord.

7 Clip the corners and neaten the seams with a zig zag stitch. Turn the cover to the right side and insert the cushion pad. Turn in the raw edge of the opening 1.3 cm (½ in) and slipstitch together for a neat finish.

Round frilled cushions

Make these as for square frilled cushions but take care when cutting out the fabric. Make a paper pattern of the size of the cushion required and use a round tray or a large plate to ensure cutting a perfect circle. From the pattern cut two circles of fabric for the top and bottom sections of the cushion cover, allowing 1.3 cm (½ in) turnings all round. Centralize patterns if necessary. Mark grain lines with tailor's tacks, or notch in four places on both top and bottom sections.

Apply the bias strip and piping cord to the front section of the cover in the same way as for the square cushion, but clip at frequent intervals to allow the piping to mould to the curved edge (*Fig 32*).

Prepare and apply the frill as for the square cushion, distributing the gathers evenly around the cushion.

When applying the back section to the front section take care to match the grain lines, using the tailor's tacks or notches made when cutting out the fabric. Leave an opening approximately 23-25.5 cm (9-10 in) long, depending on the cushion size, and finish as in 7 above.

Cushion with pleated frill

For a cushion cover with a pleated edge make up the cushion as before. Follow the instructions for making a double frill (*p. 47*) but allow three times the measurement round the four sides of the cushion.

Divide the frill into four equal sections and pleat up each section to fit into each side of the top cover section. Allow an extra pleat for each corner so that the pleating sets well. Pin and tack the pleating checking it against the top section for fit and adjusting where necessary.

With right sides together, apply the frill to the cover over the piping cord, matching the raw edges (*Fig 33*). Pin, tack and machine stitch into position using a zipper foot attachment. Clip the corners and neaten the raw edges. Turn the cover to the right side and insert the pad. Slipstitch the opening as before.

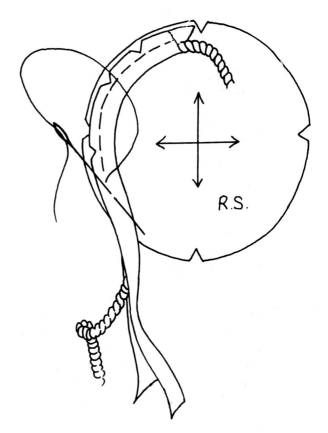

32 MARKING GRAIN LINES ON TOP AND BOTTOM SECTIONS WITH NOTCHES OR TAILOR'S TACKS

33 APPLYING THE PLEATED FRILL OVER THE PIPING CORD

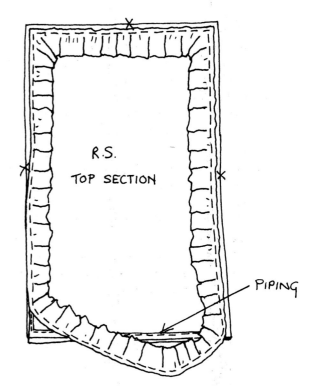

THROW-OVER BEDSPREADS

Bedcovers are important features, as they are often the focal point in a bedroom, providing the largest area of colour and texture.

Choose styles for bedspreads that suit the fabric. If a gathered frill is planned, the fabric must have good draping qualities; but for a pleated style a firmer fabric is advisable.

Throw-over bedspreads are easy to make and their success or otherwise lies in the choice of fabric. Choose firm, medium-weight fabrics that are crease-resistant and ones that can be dry-cleaned or washed easily. This is particularly important when selecting fabrics for children's bedspreads. Wide-width fabrics work well when making bedcovers as they often make joins unnecessary. Remember that random match patterns are easier to handle and there is less wastage than when using large pattern repeats.

Use throw-over bedcovers with duvets as well as with sheets and blankets, for as well as protecting it from dirt and dust they help to give the bed a neat appearance during the day.

Interesting effects can be achieved by the use of appliqué. This is especially suited to children's and teenagers' bedrooms where the theme can be carried through to the headboards, blinds or curtains. The use of simple patchwork designs can also be very successful. Traditional English quilting designs can be worked onto this type of bedspread, but whilst it is a most attractive form of decoration it is a lengthy process and requires time and patience.

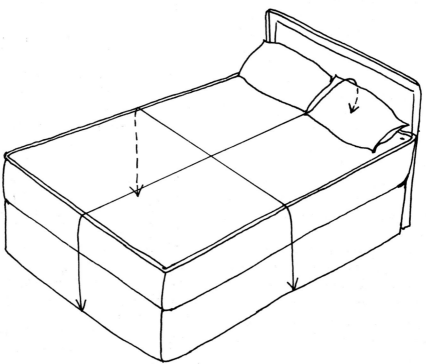

34 TAKING MEASUREMENTS OVER A MADE-UP BED

50

Measuring up

To estimate the amount of fabric needed take the measurements shown in *Fig 34* over the bed when it is made up with the usual bedclothes and pillows.

Six m (yd) of 122 cm (48 in) wide fabric is usually sufficient for a standard length bed. This would be sufficient for a single or a medium-size double bed, but more would be required for a king size bed, or when matching fabrics with large pattern repeats. Beds vary in width, length and height so check all measurements very carefully and allow enough fabric to tuck behind the pillows.

When choosing lining fabrics make sure they have the same washing or dry-cleaning qualities as those of the bedspread fabric.

Throw-over bedspreads usually finish at floor level, but if a matching or co-ordinating bed valance is used over the bed base, make the cover to finish just below its top edge. Allow 2.5 cm (1 in) turnings on all sections when making bedcovers.

1 Cut two widths of fabric to the length required. Use one width for the central section and cut the other width in half lengthwise, joining one to each side of the central section so that this is in the centre of the bed. Cut off the selvedges after matching any patterns satisfactorily. Use outside tacking for the greatest accuracy (*Fig 11*).

   For a single size bedspread the width of the central section may need to be reduced slightly to the width of the bed before the side sections are joined.

2 With right sides together make flat seams and press them open. If a lining is not being used, join the fabric with French or flat fell seams.

3 Make rounded ends at the foot of the bedcover to allow it to hang neatly. Use a large tray or plate to obtain the curved shape at each corner. Mark and cut one side first and then fold over the bedspread lengthwise and match the other side to it exactly. Notch the curves when making the hems in order to take in the extra fullness. For an unlined cover, pin and tack 1.3 cm (½ in) double hems all round the bedspread. Square corners should be mitred. Machine stitch into position.

4 To make a lining for the bedspread, cut out and seam the lining in the same way as the cover fabric. With wrong sides together apply the lining to the cover, matching seams. Lockstitch together along the seams (*Fig 9*). Trim the lining fabric to the size of the bedspread. Turn in 2.5 cm (1 in) all round and tack and slip-stitch into position.

Quilted bedspread

Throw-over bedspreads can be given more warmth and interest by inserting a thin layer of synthetic wadding between the face fabric and the lining. The use of co-ordinating fabrics makes them reversible.

Quilt the bedspread on the machine using a long straight stitch, making rows of stitching 7.5-10 cm (3-4 in) apart. First mark horizontal or diagonal guide lines from the centre of the bedspread, using long tacking stitches (*Fig 35*). Alternatively, if the fabric allows, fold and iron it concertina style to get a line for stitching. A quilting gauge when stitching helps to ensure equal distances between the lines.

To make a bound edge on the bedspread, trim the raw edges and tack the bedspread 2.5 cm (1 in) in from the raw edges. Cut bias strips 5 cm (2 in) wide in matching or co-

3 QUILTED AND FRILLED DUVET COVER AND
MATCHING PILLOWCASES

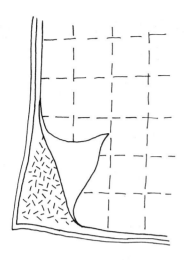

35 SANDWICHING A LAYER OF SYNTHETIC
WADDING BETWEEN TWO LAYERS OF FABRIC
AND MARKING GUIDE LINES FOR THE QUILTING
PROCESS

ordinating fabric (use the quick method on
p. 19). Pin and tack these to the right side of
the cover and machine into position. Fold
over the raw edge of the strip 1.3 cm (½ in)
and turn to the reverse side of the bedspread.
Pin and tack along the machine stitch line on
the reverse side and slipstitch into position.

Lace bedspread

White or ivory cotton lace can be used
effectively to make pretty throw-over
bedspreads. Available by the metre (yard)
and usually in 152 cm (60 in) widths as well
as 122 cm (48 in), it is ideally suited for both
single and double beds. Seams are usually
unnecessary.

1 Cut the fabric to the required length and
width and make a 2.5 cm (1 in) double
hem at the top edge.

2 If the lace has a suitable motif, cut round
this to show off the pattern, perhaps
making scalloped edges. Bind the raw

36 A BED VALANCE FITS OVER THE BASE OF THE
BED UNDERNEATH THE MATTRESS

edges with bias strips or folded bias
binding. Alternatively, decorate with a
suitable fringe or other trimming.

BED VALANCE

A bed valance (sometimes called a frill or a
flounce) fits over the base of the bed and
underneath the mattress (*Fig 36*). It protects
the base from dirt and dust but is also
decorative and hides both the legs of the bed
(if there are any) and the storage space
underneath.

Choose crease-resistant furnishing fabrics
that co-ordinate well with bedspreads,
curtains etc., or choose easy-care poly/
cotton sheetings that match duvets and fitted
sheets. The whole of the valance can be made
from poly/cotton sheeting, and as this is
easily washable it makes it a suitable choice
for children's rooms. If choosing furnishing
fabrics the frill can be lined with a curtain
lining sateen and this makes the valance
more substantial. Use calico or strong cotton
fabric for the valance base section but make
the facings from the furnishing fabric as the
edges of these sometimes show.

The amount of fabric required for a
valance depends on the size of the bed and
the height of its base as well as the style of frill

used (gathered or pleated). Usually 4½ m (4½ yd) of 122 cm (48 in) wide fabric is sufficient for a single or a medium-size double bed, but check the measurements of each bed carefully. For a gathered frill allow 1½-2 times the measurement round the base of the bed; for an inverted pleat at each corner of the foot of the bed allow the measurement round the bed plus 40.5 cm (16 in) for each pleat. The depth of the frill can vary from 30.5 cm (12 in) to 35.5 cm (15 in), depending on the height of the bed. Allow 7.5 cm (3 in) for turnings when cutting out the fabric.

Gathered valance

1 For a gathered valance in furnishing fabric cut a piece of calico the size of the base of the bed plus 2.5 cm (1 in) for turnings. Pin and tack a 1.3 cm (½ in) hem all round and machine stitch into position. This makes the edges firm.

2 For the three facings cut three strips of face fabric 15 cm (6 in) wide, two the length of the bed base and one its width. Allow 2.5 cm (1 in) for turnings on each strip when cutting out.

3 Cut out the strips of fabric for the frill, cutting it from selvedge to selvedge. Join these with 1.3 cm (½ in) turnings to obtain the required length. Press seams open. (If using poly/cotton make joins with French seams to enclose the raw edges.) Make a 1.3 cm (½ in) double hem at the two short sides of the frill and a 2.5 cm (1 in) double hem at the lower edge. These hems can be machined or stitched by hand. If lining the frill with curtain lining sateen follow the instructions for working the side and lower hems of lined curtains on p. 70.

4 Pin the facing strips to the base section

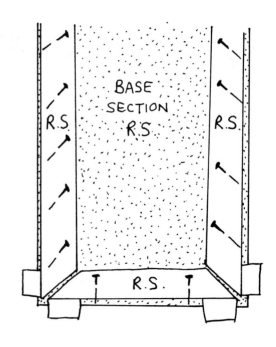

37 MITRING THE FACINGS FIRST BY PINNING THEM TO THE BASE SECTION

and mitre the two corners (*Fig 37*). Remove the facing and machine the mitred corners, leaving 1.3 cm (½ in) unstitched at each end (*Fig 38*). Fold in the edges of the facing sections 1.3 cm (½ in) and press (*Fig 39*).

5 Divide the base into six equal sections and mark these clearly with tailor's chalk.

6 For a gathered style divide the length of the frill into six equal sections and make two rows of running stitches 1.3 cm (½ in) from the top edge of each one. Draw up the gathering stitches and distribute them evenly so that they fit into each of the six sections marked on the base fabric.

7 Working on the base of the bed and with the wrong sides together, pin and tack the frill to the base section (*Fig 40*). For

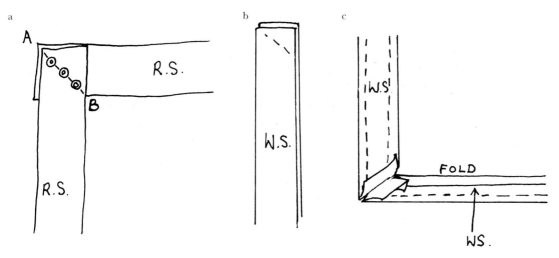

a

b

c

A

R.S.

B

R.S.

W.S.

W.S.

FOLD

WS.

38 MAKING THE MITRE ON THE FACINGS

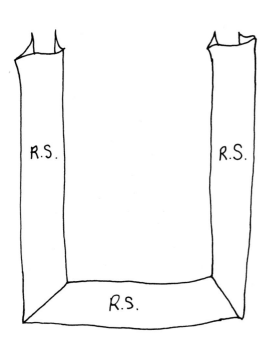

R.S.

R.S.

R.S.

39 FOLDING IN THE EDGES OF THE FACINGS
1.3 CM (½ IN), THEN PRESSING

pleated corners fold and arrange an inverted pleat at each bottom corner and tack into position with wrong sides facing.

8 To make a piped edge, cut out and prepare enough bias strips 3.8 cm (1½ in) wide to fit round the base section. Use contrasting or matching fabric. Apply the piping and bias strips to the base section, pinning and tacking over the gathered edge, taking particular care not to stretch it (*Fig 41*).

9 Pin and tack the facing to the frill over the piping, matching the mitred corners to the corners of the valance. Keep the right sides of the facing to the right side of the frill. Machine through all thicknesses along the two sides and the bottom edge of the valance. Clip corners and trim seams.

10 Lay the valance in position on the base of the bed so that it is flat. Pin and tack the folded inner edge of the facing to the base section. Remove the valance from the

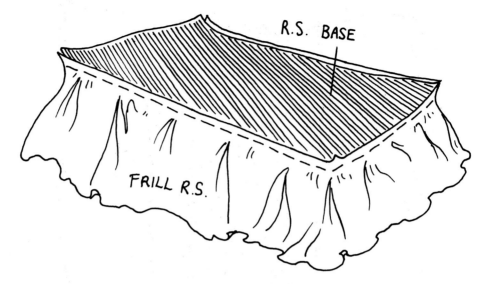

R.S. BASE

FRILL R.S.

40 PINNING AND TACKING THE WRONG SIDE OF
THE FRILL TO THE BASE SECTION

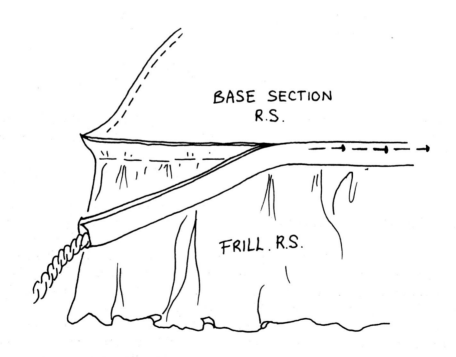

BASE SECTION
R.S.

FRILL. R.S.

41 APPLYING THE PIPING AND BIAS STRIP TO THE
BASE SECTION OVER THE FRILL

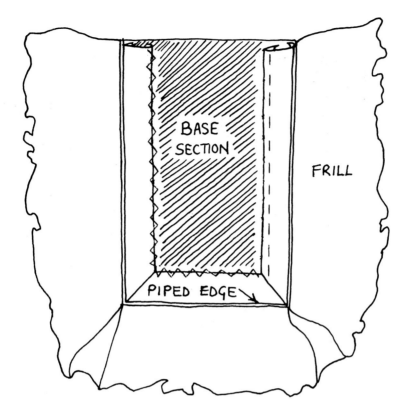

BASE SECTION

FRILL

PIPED EDGE

42 TURNING IN THE FACING ONTO THE BASE
SECTION AND MACHINING WITH A LARGE ZIG
ZAG STITCH

base of the bed and machine stitch into position using a large zig zag stitch (*Fig 42*).

PLEATED FIRM LAMPSHADE

Pleated conical shades can be made quite simply using wallpaper or other substantial papers. Alternatively, apply fabric or paper to a special PVC lampshade material which has instant adhesion on one side. This gives a more permanent result. Cut to the size required and press the fabric or paper on to its sticky surface, peeling off the protective surface as you work. Use a conical strutted frame with a plastic coating. This does not need to be bound with tape when making this style of lampshade.

Estimate the amount of paper or fabric required by measuring twice the circumference of the lower ring. This makes the most effective pleating. If necessary, joins can be made to obtain the required measurement. Make these after pleating the paper or fabric by overlapping the ends of the paper so that they are concealed inside a pleat. Secure with adhesive.

The depth of the paper should be the length of the side strut of the frame plus 5 cm (2 in). This allows for an overlap of 2.5 cm (1 in) at both the top and bottom rings (*Fig 43*).

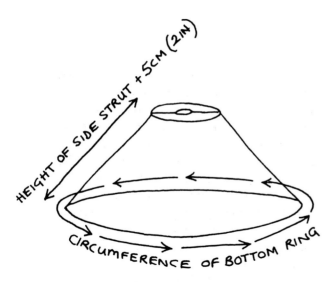

43 ESTIMATING THE REQUIREMENTS FOR A
PLEATED PAPER SHADE

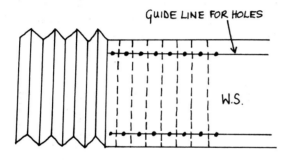

GUIDE LINE FOR HOLES

W.S.

44 FOLDING THE PAPER ALONG THE VERTICAL
GUIDE MARKS, AND PUNCHING HOLES ALONG
THE HORIZONTAL LINE

1 Cut out the paper to the required size. On the wrong side, and working from the top to the bottom of the paper, measure and draw with a faint pencil mark, accurate guide lines for the pleating; 1.9 cm (¾ in) is usually a suitable measurement for most sizes of shade but this can be varied to suit its size.

2 Draw a guide line 2.5 cm (1 in) down from the top edge of the wrong side of the paper using a faint pencil line.

3 Fold the paper carefully making concertina-like pleats following the vertical guide lines marked on the wrong side (*Fig 44*). Make any joins necessary overlapping the edges so that they are concealed in a pleat. Secure with a good quick-drying adhesive.

4 Use a hole punch to make a hole in the centre of each pleat using the guide line marked 2.5 cm (1 in) from the top edge. Thread a narrow ribbon or cord through the holes and draw up the pleating until it fits snugly over the top edge of the frame. Make sure that the pleats are arranged evenly around the frame and tie a bow or a knot to finish (*Fig 45*). To secure the shade more firmly to the frame, weave a length of thread around the cord and the top ring (*Fig 46*).

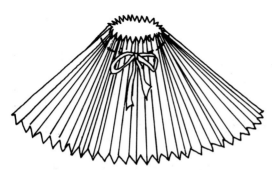

45 ARRANGING THE PLEATS CAREFULLY AND
TYING UP WITH A KNOT OR A BOW

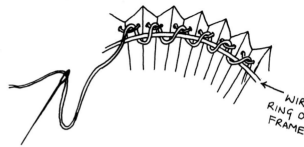

46 SECURING THE SHADE TO THE FRAME BY
WEAVING THREAD AROUND THE CORD AND
THE TOP RING

TABLECLOTHS

Small chipboard tables look attractive when covered with circular cloths draped to the floor, and these provide useful bedside or display tables. Smaller circular or square cloths in co-ordinating fabric can be made for covering the top, or a lace tablecloth can be used for a pretty country style. If necessary, protect and cover the cloth with a piece of glass cut to the size of the table top.

Make tablecloths for bedside tables in plain or co-ordinating fabrics to mix and match with curtains, bedcovers etc. These can be lined and interlined as necessary and decorated with frills or other trimmings (follow the instructions for lined and interlined curtains on pp 70 and 95). Alternatively, the edges may be bound with a simple bias strip made in a contrasting fabric.

To estimate the amount of fabric required find the centre of the table and, with a tape or rigid rule, measure from this point down to the floor (or to the required length for the tablecloth). This is the radius (*Fig 47*). Double this measurement to obtain the diameter of the tablecloth. If this figure is greater than the width of the fabric then it will be necessary to join fabric widths together before the circle of material is cut out. A square of fabric of the diameter is required.

Buy the widest fabric possible in order to avoid the necessity for seams. For a floor-length cloth, however, these are usually necessary. Make the seams at the sides so that they are as inconspicuous as possible (*Fig 48*) and match any patterns carefully using outside tacking (*Fig 11*).

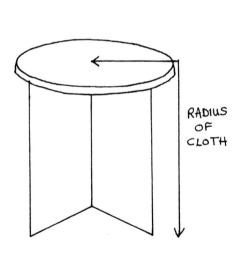

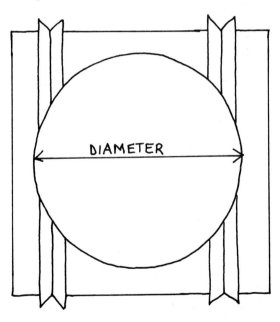

47 MEASURING THE TABLE TO ESTIMATE FABRIC REQUIREMENTS

48 CUTTING OUT THE TABLECLOTH FROM A SQUARE OF FABRIC; JOINS IN THE FABRIC SHOULD BE MADE AT THE SIDE OF A CENTRAL PANEL

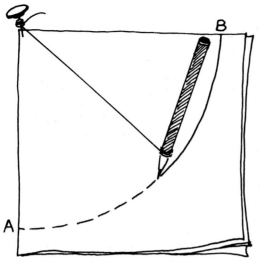

49 MAKING THE PATTERN FOR A CIRCULAR
TABLECLOTH

50 NOTCHING THE EDGE OF THE CLOTH BEFORE
TURNING OVER THE HEM

Circular tablecloth

1 To cut out a circle make a paper pattern first to the size required. Take a square piece of newspaper or brown paper large enough to make the circle (join it with sticky tape to obtain the size required). Fold it in four so that each side of the square measures a little more than the radius of the tablecloth.

2 Tie one end of a piece of string to a pencil as near to its point as possible. Take the radius measurement of the tablecloth and mark this on the string with a drawing pin. Secure the drawing pin at this point into one corner of the folded paper. Holding the pencil upright draw an arc from A to B, keeping the string taut (*Fig 49*). Cut out along the pencil line through all thicknesses of the paper to obtain the circle.

3 Fold the square of fabric for the tablecloth lengthwise and cut out the fabric using one half of the paper pattern set against the fold. If the cloth is very large, fold the fabric both lengthwise and widthwise and use one quarter of the pattern only to cut out the fabric (set against both folds).

4 Finish the edges of the tablecloth with frills or other trimmings, first making a narrow hem and neatening the raw edges with bias binding. Alternatively, bind the raw edges with bias strips using a co-ordinating or contrasting fabric. Prepare enough bias strips to fit round the edge of the cloth, using the quick method described on p. 19.

5 For a neat hem, notch the cloth at the raw edges making these 1.3 cm (½ in) deep and approximately 2.5 cm (1 in) apart (*Fig 50*). Pin and tack bias binding to the raw edge and machine into position. Trim the seam to 6 mm (¼ in) and fold over the bias binding to the wrong side of the cloth. Tack into position and either hemstitch by hand or machine stitch the binding into place (*Fig. 51*).

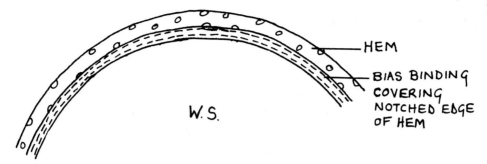

W. S.

51 MACHINE STITCHING THE BIAS BINDING
TO THE HEM

FABRIC-COVERED PHOTOGRAPH FRAMES

Attractive fabric-covered frames can be made for photographs of all sizes using lightweight furnishing fabrics, dress cottons and silks. Choose closely-woven fabrics made from natural fibres where possible, as these fold well and are easy to use. Man-made fibres are more difficult to handle than natural ones. With fine fabrics such as silk, use a very thin layer of synthetic wadding behind the fabric to give it a slightly padded finish. Use acetate film to protect the photographs. This can be obtained from good art shops.

Make single and double photograph frames following the instructions below. These can be adapted for use with any size of photograph.

Single photograph frame (16.5 x 12.5 cm [6½ x 5 in])

1 Cut out three pieces of stiff card (cereal packet thickness) 16.5 x 12.5 cm (6½ x 5 in) and mark them 'front', 'middle' and 'back'. Using the 'front' section of card, cut out a window 2.5 cm (1 in) from the edge using a craft knife or a very sharp pair of scissors, taking care to obtain a sharp cut at the four corners. On the 'back' section of card score a line with a sharp knife 5 cm (2 in) down from the top edge from side to side (Fig 52).

2 Cut out three pieces of fabric 21.5 x 18 cm (8½ x 7 in) to cover the three pieces of card.

3 Place a piece of fabric right side down and lay the back section on top with the scored side uppermost. Mitre the corner (Fig 52), cutting off part of the mitre to make the corner less bulky. Secure the fabric firmly

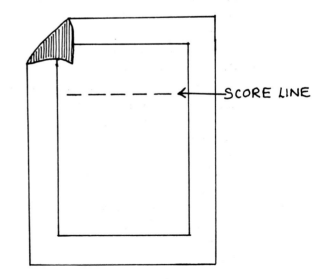

SCORE LINE

52 MARKING A SCORE LINE ON THE BACK
SECTION AND MITRING THE CORNERS

61

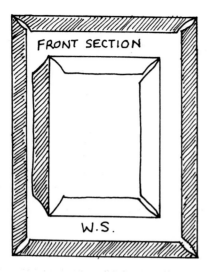

FRONT SECTION

W.S.

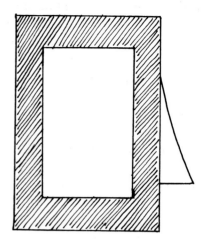

53 FOLDING AND SECURING THE FABRIC TO THE
FRONT SECTION

54 FABRIC-COVERED PHOTOGRAPH FRAME

in place with a quick-drying adhesive. Cut a sheet of good-quality writing paper to the size of the back section and apply to the wrong side of the card over the raw edges of the fabric.

4 Cover the middle section with fabric and paper in the same way as the back section. Place the middle and back sections together with paper sides facing and apply adhesive from the top edge down to the score line for 5 cm (2 in).

5 Apply the cover fabric to the front section in the same way as for the back, but when the outer edges have been secured with adhesive cut out a small rectangle in the middle of the fabric. Trim and fold to the wrong side (*Fig 53*), and secure with adhesive.

6 Place the front section to the middle and back sections, spreading the adhesive in a 6 mm (¼ in) strip round the two sides and bottom edges of the middle section. Leave the top edge open so that the photograph can be inserted.

7 Cut a piece of acetate film slightly smaller than the size of the frame and insert between the front and middle sections to protect the photographs (*Fig 54*).

Double photograph frame (25.5 x 12.5 cm [10 x 5 in])

1 Cut four pieces of card 12.5 x 12.5 cm (5 x 5 in). On two pieces of the card measure and draw a line 2.5 cm (1 in) from each edge and cut out a window 7.5 x 7.5 cm (3 x 3 in). Cut two pieces of cover fabric 15 x 15 cm (6 x 6 in) and lay the pieces of card onto the fabric with right sides facing. Fold over the fabric at the outer edges and mitre the corners (*Fig 52*). Secure with adhesive. Cut out the fabric in the middle of the window, trim and fold to the wrong side (*Fig 53*) and secure with adhesive.

2 Cut a strip of fabric 1.9 cm (¾ in) wide and 12.5 cm (5 in) long and with this join the two plain pieces of card together using

adhesive. Leave a gap of approximately 6 mm (¼ in) between the two pieces so that the photograph frame will fold (*Fig 55*).

3 Cut a piece of cover fabric 15 x 29 cm (6 x 11½ in). Place the back sections onto the wrong side of the fabric and fold over the edges 1.3 cm (½ in) and mitre each corner as before. Secure with adhesive (*Fig 56*).

4 Place the two front window sections to the wrong side of the back section (*Fig 57*), applying 6 mm (¼ in) strips of adhesive round the two sides and lower edges. Leave the top edges open for the insertion of the photographs.

5 Cut two pieces of acetate film slightly smaller than the frames and insert them between the front and back sections to protect the photographs.

HERB CUSHIONS AND LAVENDER/POT POURRI SACHETS

Pretty 'boudoir' cushions can be made in various shapes and sizes and filled with sweet-scented herbs, lavender or pot pourri. Dry the lavender by hanging in bunches upside down with a paper bag tied round the flowers. When dry they will fall into the paper bag. Do not use a plastic bag as this will not allow the air to circulate. Herbs to use are marjoram, meadowsweet, lemon verbena, rosemary, thyme, hops and rosebuds. Herb pillows are a pleasant way of inducing sleep and they add a touch of luxury to the bedroom.

Choose satins, silks, fine cottons and lace for best effects, or match or co-ordinate the cushions to other bed linen, using polyester/cotton sheeting with small designs. Trim the

55 JOINING THE TWO BACK SECTIONS WITH A STRIP OF FABRIC

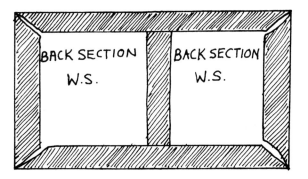

56 COVERING THE BACK SECTIONS WITH FABRIC

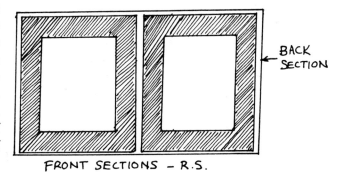

57 PLACING THE FRONT WINDOW SECTIONS TO THE BACK SECTION

cushions with lace or frills or use pin tucking or quilting as surface decoration.

Heart-shaped herb cushion

1 Cut out a paper pattern of a heart to the size required and add 1.3 cm (½ in) turnings. The filling will take up some of the fabric so cut the pattern slightly larger to allow for this. Other simple shapes can be used such as triangles, diamonds and shells.

2 Make an inner pad to the same shape, using fine lawn or muslin and synthetic wadding as a filling. Sprinkle the herbs or lavender between three or four layers of wadding to make a sandwich. Oversew round the edges to hold the layers in place and slip it into the inner case. Oversew the opening. This method of filling means that the herbs do not show through the face fabric and that the cushion has a smooth appearance when finished.

3 Make the outer cover for the cushion following the instructions on p. 47, but instead of piping use lace or frills to give the cushion a luxurious look.

Lavender/pot pourri sachets

Use these sachets to hang from the covered coat-hangers on p. 65.

1 Cut two pieces of fabric 10 x 7.5 cm (4 x 3 in) to match or co-ordinate with the coat-hanger. With right sides together, tack and machine the two sides and the lower edge allowing 6 mm (¼ in) turnings. Snip corners and turn the right sides out. Cut along the top edge of the bag with pinking shears.

2 Fill the bag with dried lavender flowers or pot pourri. Enclose these with a row of

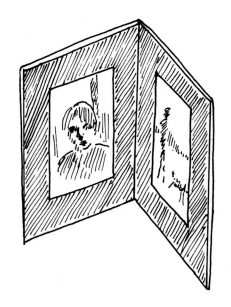

58 DOUBLE PHOTOGRAPH FRAME COVERED IN FABRIC

59 HEART-SHAPED HERB CUSHION

1 AN UNLINED FESTOON BLIND LETS LIGHT
THROUGH AND ADDS A PRETTY TOUCH

2 THE CO-ORDINATED CURTAINS, BEDCOVER AND
BOLSTER CUSHION ARE COMPLEMENTED BY THE
GRACEFUL BED CANOPY

3 THE PRETTY FRILLED DUVET COVER AND
PILLOWCASES HAVE A CONTRASTING BED VALANCE
AND CURTAIN

4 THE GRACEFUL BED CANOPY AND CURTAINS
WITH DECORATIVE VALANCE AND TIE-BACKS
COMPLEMENT THE SMART PIPED EDGES OF THE
CUSHIONS AND BED COVER

5 FRILLED CUSHIONS ADD A FINAL LUXURIOUS
TOUCH

6 THE CO-ORDINATED QUILTED BED COVER,
VALANCE, HEADBOARD AND CURTAINS MAKE AN
ELEGANT BEDROOM SETTING

7 THESE LUXURIOUS FULL-LENGTH CURTAINS
WITH PLEATED VALANCE, HAVE THEIR DESIGN
PICKED OUT IN THE WALL STENCIL

1 Remove the seal on the tip of the crayon by drawing a cross onto a paper towel

2 Position the first stencil sheet in place and secure with low tack tape; rub paint from the crayon onto an uncut area of the stencil

3 With a circular motion work all the paint well into the bristles of the brush

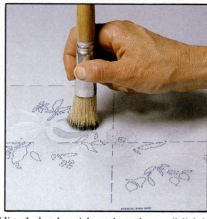

4 Holding the brush at right angles to the stencil, lightly apply paint to the cutout areas using large clockwise and anti-clockwise circular movements

5 For darker shading simply repeat. Repeat the process with the second sheet, using a different colour

6 The end result—a beautiful stencil—with no smudges, drips or paint runs

60 SMALL LAVENDER/POT POURRI SACHETS

running stitches worked 3.2 cm (1¼ in) from the top of the bag. Gather up and secure with a few stitches.

3 Tie a small piece of satin ribbon 6 mm (¼ in) wide round the top of the bag and sew to the hanger (*Fig 61*).

Alternatively, small sachets can be made using simple shapes such as hearts and circles. Fill them with lavender or pot pourri and hang them from coat-hangers with pieces of satin ribbon.

COVERED COAT-HANGERS

These padded coat-hangers help clothes to keep their shape well. They are also attractive additions to any wardrobe and they make delightful gifts. Choose lightweight furnishing or dress fabrics such as satins and silks and add a sweet smelling sachet to finish. Approximately 0.5 m (½ yd) of fabric covers four average-size coat-hangers. Use strips of bump or domette left over from other projects to bind the

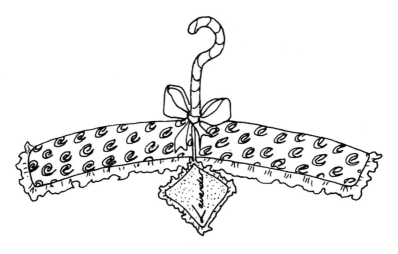

61 PADDED COAT HANGER WITH DECORATIVE
RIBBON AND LAVENDER BAG

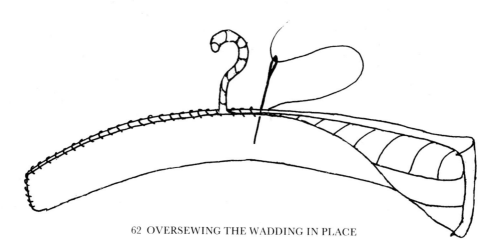

62 OVERSEWING THE WADDING IN PLACE

hanger, or any other soft fabric that is available.

1 Cut a strip of cover fabric 45.5 cm (18 in) by 1.3 m (½ in) wide to bind the metal hook. Fold in and press 3 mm (⅛ in) along one long side of the strip. Bind the hook with the fabric, overlapping it so that the raw edges are enclosed. Apply a little adhesive to the metal to hold it firmly in place. Wind the strip round the hanger at the bottom of the hook and secure with a few stitches.

2 Bind the hanger with a strip of bump or domette (or other soft fabric). Cut a piece 5 cm (2 in) wide and 2½ times the length of the hanger. Use a little adhesive on the wooden part of the hanger to secure it firmly. Finish with a few stitches to hold it in place.

3 Cut a piece of synthetic wadding the length of the hanger plus 2.5 cm (1 in), and 45.5 x 10 cm (18 x 4 in) wide. Fold this in half lengthwise and place round the hanger, turning in each end 1.3 cm (½ in). Oversew along the top edge (*Fig 62*).

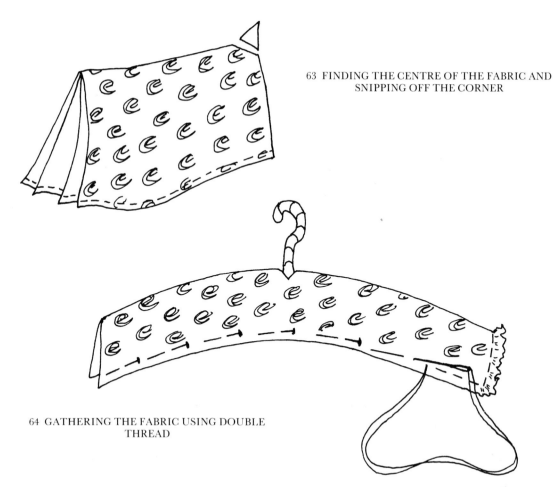

64 GATHERING THE FABRIC USING DOUBLE
THREAD

4 Cut a piece of fabric 48.5 x 18 cm
(19 x 7 in) for the cover. Turn in a 6 mm
(¼) double hem all round on the wrong
side of the fabric. Machine stitch into
position and press.

5 Find the centre of the fabric by folding
first in half lengthwise and then in
quarters. Make a hole in the centre of the
fabric by snipping off the corner (*Fig 63*).
Slip the cover over the hanger with the
hook going through the hole.

6 Pin the machined edges together and sew
with a running stitch using matching
double thread, gathering where necessary
to take in any fullness. This is particularly
necessary at each end of the hanger
(*Fig 64*).

7 Tie a bow of satin ribbon round the hook.
Make a lavender or pot pourri sachet
(*p. 64*) and attach securely with a few
stitches to the lower edge of the hanger.
Tie a matching bow at the top of the
sachet.

WASTEPAPER BINS AND COTTON WOOL HOLDERS

Choose large drum-shaped tins or uncovered
wastebins sold ready to cover. These are
usually available in large department stores.
Alternatively, cover an existing drum-
shaped bin.

For small cotton wool holders and soap
tidies cover smaller cans (e.g. soup, baked

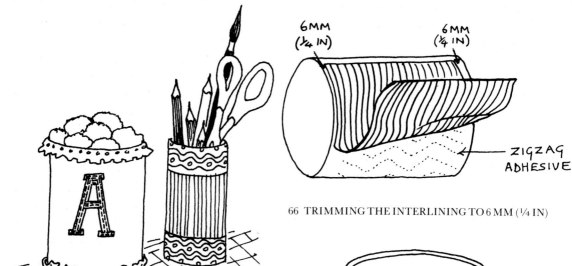

66 TRIMMING THE INTERLINING TO 6 MM (¼ IN)

6MM
(¼ IN)

6MM
(¼ IN)

ZIGZAG
ADHESIVE

65 FABRIC-COVERED CANISTERS

bean cans etc.). These tidies can be made
very successfully from small pieces of fabric
left over from other projects, including
broderie Anglaise or lace etc., trimmed with
ribbons and bows. These co-ordinate well
with many fabrics and also make most
attractive gifts, particularly when combined
with other small accessories such as padded
hangers, tissue boxes etc.

If covering food cans, make quite sure that
there are no rough edges at the top. If
necessary, cover these with a length of bias
strip 3.8 cm (1½ in) wide. Paint the inside of
the can with a quick-drying enamel or gloss
paint and allow to dry thoroughly before
using.

1 Measure the depth of the can and its
circumference to estimate the amount of
fabric required. Cut a piece of interlining
such as bump or domette to these
measurements.

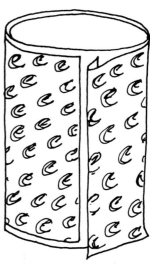

67 TURNING IN THE RAW EDGE 1.3 CM (½ IN)

2 For the face fabric cut out a piece to the
above measurements but add 2.5 cm
(1 in) to the circumference measurements
for turning allowance. Cut out the fabric
so that the selvedge runs from the top to
the bottom of the can.

3 Turn the bin onto its side to apply the
interlining. Trim the interlining so that
there will be a 6 mm (¼ in) gap at both top
and bottom edges of the bin. This fabric
gives a slightly padded look to the

wastepaper bin or tidy and improves the finished result. Apply a suitable adhesive in zig zag fashion from the top to the bottom of the bin and apply the interlining to it, making sure that it is at right angles to the top edge (*Fig 66*). If there is a seam where the metal is joined, use this as a guide line to get a straight edge. Do not overlap the interlining at its join but trim the raw edges and butt them together.

4 Apply the face fabric to the bin in the same way as the interlining but apply adhesive to the top and lower edges only. Make sure that the fabric is firmly positioned and that the grain line is straight. Finish the join by turning in 1.3 cm (½ in) and overlap onto the raw edge (*Fig 67*).

5 Cover the raw edges at the top and bottom of the bin with braid, velvet ribbon or other decorative trimming. Do not apply this to the seam line.

Add interest to these bins and tidies by decorating the face fabric where suitable with beads, sequins, appliqué or other embroidery before it is applied to the bin. This is a useful way of treating bins in children's bedrooms, and study/bedrooms. Embroidered initials and monograms are also effective.

SEVEN

Plain and tailored bedroom

•

LINED CURTAINS

Most curtains are enhanced by a lining. As well as helping the curtain to drape well it protects the curtain fabric from sunlight, frost and dust, all of which damage the fibres of the fabric. This makes it wear out more quickly.

Choose a good-quality curtain lining sateen. Do not try to pull a thread to straighten the edge, but cut out each length against a square table, or using a set square. As lining sateen is not evenly woven, do not try to tear it.

Stitch lined curtains by hand except when working the long seams that join the fabric widths together and when applying the heading tapes, which, when tacked, are best machine stitched into position.

Remember to check that the lining sateen is the same width as the curtain fabric. If not, separate calculations will be necessary when estimating fabric requirements.

Lock the lining to the curtain fabric to ensure that it hangs well and does not fall away from the curtain fabric. Locking stitches are long loose stitches made so that they do not pull and therefore pucker the curtain when it is hanging.

Lined curtain with pencil pleating

1 Estimate the amount of fabric required, (*p. 35*) and cut out the curtain. Match any patterns carefully using outside tacking (*Fig 11*) and then cut off the selvedges or snip them to prevent the seams from puckering. Join widths or half widths of fabric with a plain flat seam and press open (*Fig 12*). It is not necessary to neaten the edges.

2 Fold in 3.8 cm (1½ in) at the sides and lower edges of the curtain and tack. Mitre the two lower corners (*Fig 16*) and slipstitch. Using matching single thread, serge stitch (*Fig 7*) the two side hems and the lower hem.

3 Cut out the lining sateen to the same measurement as the curtain fabric, removing all selvedges. Join widths or half widths as necessary using a plain flat seam. Press open.

4 Press the face fabric of the curtain carefully before applying the lining sateen and then lay it onto a large table with the wrong side uppermost. Press the lining and apply it to the curtain fabric with wrong sides together. Match the seams of the lining to the seams of the curtain where possible.

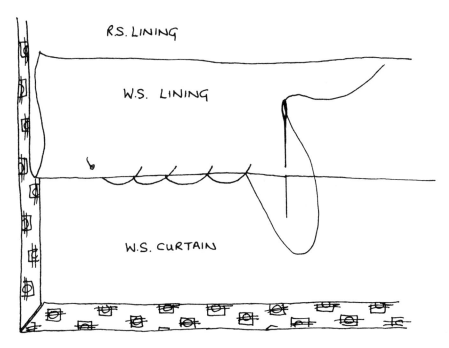

R.S. LINING

W.S. LINING

W.S. CURTAIN

68 LOCKING THE LINING TO THE CURTAIN
FABRIC WITH A LONG LOOSE STITCH

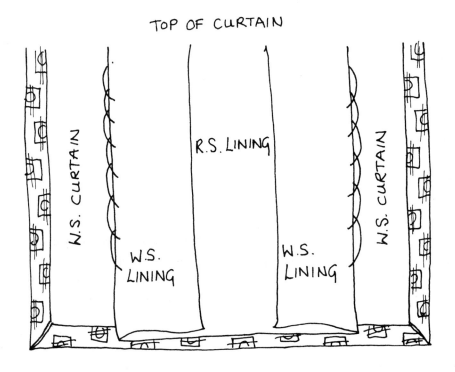

TOP OF CURTAIN

W.S. CURTAIN

R.S. LINING

W.S.
LINING

W.S.
LINING

W.S. CURTAIN

69 LOCKSTITCHING THE LINING DOWN THE
LENGTH OF THE CURTAIN

5 Lock the lining to the curtain fabric (*Figs 9 and 68*). Two to three rows of locking stitches should be made in every width of 122 cm (48 in) fabric. Work these from the top to the bottom of the curtain length, matching the thread to the curtain fabric. Start by folding back the lining at the centre of the curtain and lock into position, making stitches every 10-15 cm (4-6 in) (*Fig 69*).

6 Trim off the lining at the side edges of the curtain so that it is level with the curtain, and fold it in 2.5 cm (1 in) at the lower and side edges. Make sure that the corner of the lining meets the mitre on the curtain as this makes a neat finish (*Fig 70*). Tack into position.

7 Work a row of tacking stitches across the curtain width 15-20.5 cm (6-8 in) from the top edge. This keeps the lining firmly in position whilst the heading is worked.

8 Slipstitch the lining to the curtain at the two sides and the lower edge using matching thread. Leave the top 15-20.5 cm (6-8 in) of the curtain unstitched to allow for the heading to be finished (*Fig 70*).

9 Apply heading tape as required. For standard pocketed heading tape see p. 45. Alternatively, apply a pencil pleated heading for a tailored, smart look. This tape is approximately 7.5 cm (3 in) deep and has a special thread woven into it that keeps the heading upright and permanently stiffened. It requires 2¼-2½ times the width of the track when estimating fabric requirements. This tape is suitable for most

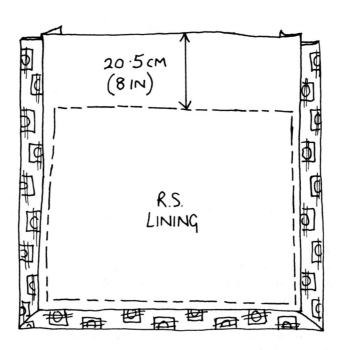

70 LEAVING THE TOP EDGE OF THE CURTAIN UNSTITCHED TO ALLOW FOR THE HEADING TO BE WORKED

weights of fabrics and has two rows of suspension pockets for the hooks which makes it suitable for use on most types of tracks or poles.

10 To apply the tape to the curtain, measure and cut the required length allowing 3.8 cm (1½ in) at each end for turnings. Pull out the pleating cords 3.8 cm (1½ in) at one end and knot each one firmly. Turn under the end of the tape and apply to the curtain 6 mm (¼ in) from the top edge. At the other end of the curtain pull out the cords ready for pleating up the curtain. Turn in the end of the tape and pin and tack it into position.

As there will be a right- and a left-hand curtain take care to apply the tape so that the loose ends of the cord are at the outer edge of each curtain. Make sure that the tape is applied with the hook pockets in their correct position (i.e. facing) and that the stitching is worked along the guide lines indicated on the tape.

As with all tapes, make the two rows of machine stitching in the same direction to prevent puckering. Stitch along the side edges of the tape taking care not to machine over the loose cords.

LINED STIFFENED PELMETS

Like curtain valances, pelments are decorative features. They came into fashion in the seventeenth century and were developed from the valance because of the changes in window design. In recent years the pelmet has lost favour to decorative curtain headings, but well-designed ones can add interest and originality to a decorative scheme. They are practical, too, since they protect curtains from dirt and dust as well as concealing the tracks and fittings.

The shape of a pelmet can alter the appearance of a window. Fix it higher than the window frame to make the window appear taller, or extend it at each side to make it appear wider. A simple pelmet provides a formal elegant mood and this style is well suited to the plain and tailored look of a masculine bedroom, a study or a town apartment.

A pelmet is usually made to match or co-ordinate with the curtains and is constructed from a special pelmet buckram. This is a coarse canvas impregnated with glue. It is sold by the metre (yard) in narrow widths so joins do not need to be made to obtain the required length. Regular buckram is also suitable and can be used with an adhesive.

Stiffened pelmets should be fixed to a pelmet board and cannot be attached to a valance rail. A pelmet board should be approximately 10 cm (4 in) deep by 2.5 cm (1 in) thick and should extend 5-7.5 cm (2-3 in) beyond the end of the curtain track. Fit it like a shelf using brackets. The height of fixing above the window frame can be varied but usually this is approximately 5-7.5 cm (2-3 in) above the frame. The pelmet is then attached to the front edge of the board using a touch and close fastening.

Pelmets are economical to make and they can considerably reduce the cost of curtaining a window, since only a gathered heading is necessary. (This requires less fullness than other decorative headings and so less fabric is needed.) They cannot be washed because of their buckram content but regular brushing or vacuuming should keep them in good condition for several years.

Estimate the fabric required by measuring the length of the pelmet board from wall to wall, remembering to include the 10 cm (4 in) return at each end. To this measurement add 5 cm (2 in) for turnings. The depth of the pelmet is determined by the design; allow 3.8 cm (1½ in) pelmet to 30.5 cm (12 in) of curtain drop, or one sixth of the total depth of floor-length curtains. To this add 10 cm (4 in) for turnings. In rooms with low ceilings keep the depth of the pelmet to a minimum but not usually less than 18 cm (7 in).

Centre the width of the fabric in the middle of the pelmet and add any extra fabric to each side of this width; never have a seam at the centre of the pelmet. When estimating the amount of fabric required remember to allow for pattern matching. The same amount of lining sateen and interlining is needed as for the face fabric. Interlining gives more body to the fabric and a slightly padded look to the pelmet.

To design the pelmet

1 Make a template of the design required, bearing in mind the following important points.

(*a*) The position where the curtains will hang when drawn back gives the measurement of the 'end' sections.

(*b*) The return at each end should be the same depth as the 'end' sections.

(*c*) The narrowest part of the pelmet must not allow the track to show when the curtains are drawn back.

2 Make a mark at the centre of the pelmet design and cut out the template in stiff paper or newspaper to the full size of the pelmet (stick or pin strips together). Mark out the important measurements and design the pelmet from the centre using plates or trays as guides to draw round. Fix the pattern onto the pelmet board with sticky tape and adjust one side of the pattern only until the required effect is achieved. Live with the paper template for a few days before cutting out the buckram, to be sure that it satisfies the eye. Fold the template in half and cut the other side to match. Use this to cut out the buckram.

If in doubt about a design, keep it simple – or straight. Pelmets can be decorated with fringe, piping cord or other decorative edges to add extra interest.

To make the pelmet

1 Cut a strip of buckram the exact length of the pelmet board (including the returns at each end). If it is necessary to join it, overlap the two edges 1.3 cm (½ in) and machine stitch into position.

2 Lay the template on the buckram and secure it by damping the buckram very slightly and ironing the paper pattern to it. Cut out the buckram shape.

Preparing the face fabric

1 Cut a strip of fabric 10 cm (4 in) larger all round than the exact size of the buckram shape. This allows for generous turnings.

2 Join widths of fabric where necessary, keeping a full width of fabric at the centre of the pelmet. Make 1.3 cm (½ in) seams, matching patterns carefully and using outside tacking (*Fig 11*). Press seams open.

Interlining

1 Cut a strip of interlining 5 cm (2 in) larger than the size of the buckram shape, joining pieces with a lapped seam and two rows of zig zag machine stitching.

2 Place the buckram onto the interlining in the centre. Starting at the top edge of the pelmet, dampen the buckram at the edges with a small cloth. Fold over the interlining and press firmly to the buckram with a hot iron. Continue in this way all round the pelmet shape, slashing curves and cutting away surplus fabric on the convex curves. Right-angled curves also need slashing. (When using regular buckram apply a little adhesive before folding over the interlining.)

Face fabric

1 Lay the pelmet shape onto the wrong side of the face fabric (*Fig 71*) and fold it over along the top edge, making sure that the fabric is correctly positioned on the right side. Dampen the buckram and press in the same way as for the interlining, slashing curves and mitring each corner.

If the fabric frays easily, reinforce each slash with a few buttonhole stitches (*Fig 72*).

2 If a decorative trimming or piping is used, this should be stitched to the pelmet before the lining is applied. With the right side of the pelmet facing, stab stitch the trimming to the pelmet using matching thread (*Fig 73*). Furnishing cords or braids can also be used on the right side of the pelmet and for a more permanent result these should be stitched on where possible and not applied with an adhesive. Buttons can be covered in the face fabric (or a contrasting one) and applied to the right side of the pelmet for decoration. Alternatively, motifs of patchwork or other decorative embroidery could be used.

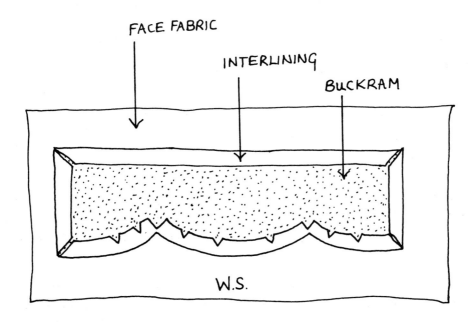

71 LAYING THE PELMET SHAPE ONTO THE WS
OF THE FACE FABRIC

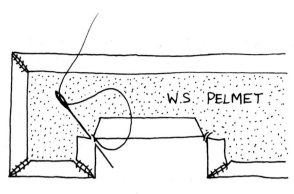

72 RE-INFORCING SLASHES WITH BUTTONHOLE
STITCHES

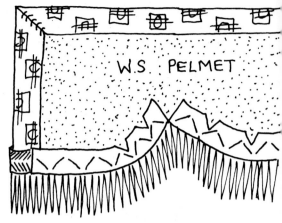

73 STITCHING THE TRIMMING TO THE PELMET
BEFORE THE LINING IS APPLIED

74 PINNING THE TOUCH AND CLOSE FASTENING
TO THE TOP EDGE OF THE PELMET

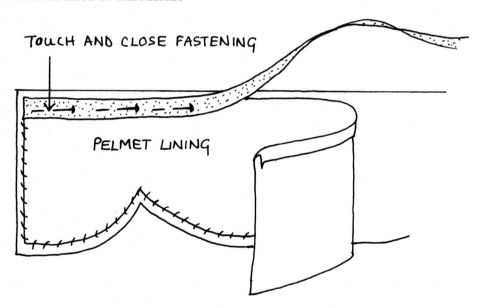

Lining

1 Cut a strip of lining sateen 5 cm (2 in) larger than the pelmet shape, joining strips if necessary with 1.3 cm (½ in) turnings and pressing seams open. Turn in 1.3 cm (½ in) along the top edge and press. Apply to the pelmet 6 mm (¼ in) from the top edge, pinning and slip-stitching into position. Cut the lining to the shaped edge, slashing where necessary, and turn in the sides and finish in the same way.

2 Cut a length of touch and close fastening to the measurement of the pelmet. Use the 'stick and sew' type, applying the adhesive side to the pelmet board. (For extra strength secure the tape further by stapling it to the board using a staple gun every 12.5-15 cm [5-6 in] along its length.) Pin the matching strip to the top edge of the pelmet (*Fig 74*) and slipstitch firmly in position all round.

ROLLER BLINDS

Roller blinds are easy and inexpensive to make and are a very practical choice for bedrooms and bathrooms. They roll right up to the top of the window round a wooden or aluminium roller and give the maximum amount of light by day. They can also be used in front of shelves in bedroom/studies as a convenient method of covering storage space for clothes, books, toys etc.

Roller blind kits are available at department stores, DIY shops and most good wallpaper shops. A kit consists of a wooden or aluminium roller with a spring and metal cap at one end and a metal cap with a pin to fix on to the other end of the roller. This has to be cut to the exact size required. Two metal brackets are also supplied to fix the blind to the window area. Follow the manufacturers instructions for fitting these. Small tacks are provided for applying the fabric to the roller and also included is a pull cord and fitting together with a wooden batten which gives weight to the bottom edge of the blind.

Specially stiffened blind fabrics in a variety of colours and patterns are available to make the blind and this is easy to use as it does not fray at the edges. It repels dirt and dust and can be sponged clean. It is made in wide widths so joining is often unnecessary. Alternatively, use closely-woven furnishing cottons, lace or nets for making roller blinds, but these need to be strengthened first with a special fabric stiffener. This can either be sprayed on to the fabric from an aerosol can or the fabric can be dipped into a liquid stiffener (usually obtainable where the kits are sold). Test a small piece of fabric first to check how much stiffening is required. As the fabric may shrink, stiffen it first before cutting it to the size required.

Make the blind from one width of fabric if possible. For a wide window the fabric can be used sideways if the pattern allows, but if necessary, make two or even three blinds for a very wide window to avoid the necessity for seams. These are not very satisfactory as they make the fabric too thick and make it more difficult for it to roll smoothly round the roller. Commercially stiffened fabrics do not fray and therefore it is not necessary to have side hems, but when a DIY fabric stiffener is used on certain sheer fabrics, it may be necessary to turn in side hems of 1.3 cm (½ in). Machine these into position using a zig zag stitch (or two rows of straight stitch). When machining take care to keep the fabric as flat as possible as the stiffened fabric can crack if folded.

The lower edge of the blind may be finished in many ways. A shaped edge can be made and fixed to the bottom edge, or a decorative braid or fringe may be used. Pull cords are available in various styles or a handmade knotted or plaited cord could be applied.

Stencilling

Decorate plain blinds with fabric paints using pre-cut stencilling packs. These border

4 MATERIALS FOR STENCILLING

designs are most effective when used in this way and may be chosen to co-ordinate with other soft furnishings, wallpapers etc. Many different designs are available for every style of room and the stencils last indefinitely.

Use specialist stencil brushes made from natural bristles to apply the fabric paint. This oil-based paint is now available in crayon form making it very easy to achieve good results. Its ease of application reduces the risk of smudging and paint runs. Packs of stencils, brushes and paints are available from department stores and most good specialist paint and wallpaper shops.

Secure the stencil to the blind using low-tack tape or masking tape before painting on the design. Practise stencilling first on a small piece of blind fabric before painting the design on to the blind.

The same method can be used for stencilling onto firm lampshades to create an unusual and original piece of work.

Making the blind

1 Decide whether the blind is to be fixed inside or outside the window recess. Fit the two brackets and cut the roller to the correct size to fit between these brackets. If a kit is not available in the exact size, buy the next one up and trim the roller to the size required.

2 Cut the fabric to the exact size of the roller. If hems need to be made at each side, a 2.5 cm (1 in) allowance must be made for these. Cut the fabric approximately 15 cm (6 in) longer than the measurement of the window. This allows for turnings at the bottom edge of the blind and also enables the fabric to be rolled round the roller at the top edge when it is pulled down the window. Take care to cut the fabric accurately otherwise the blind will not roll evenly. Square up the fabric with the edge of a table or use a T-square to get accurate angles.

3 At the lower edge turn up 1.3 cm (½ in) to the wrong side of the blind and then turn over 3.8 cm (1½ in) to make a casing for the wooden batten. Use a little adhesive to hold the hem in place and then machine along the hem using a large zig zag stitch (*Fig 75*).

4 Position the blind to the roller (*Fig 76*) making sure that the right side is uppermost. Place the fabric to the guide line on the roller and stick down with a little adhesive. Knock in small tacks every 3.8 cm (1½ in) along the roller.

5 Cut the wooden batten to the width of the blind and insert it in the casing at the lower edge. Knot one end of the pull cord and thread through the acorn fitting. Screw the fitment to the wrong side of the blind, (*Fig 77*). Decorate the lower edge of

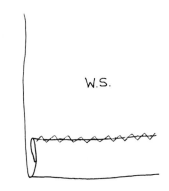

75 MAKING A CASING AT THE LOWER EDGE OF THE BLIND

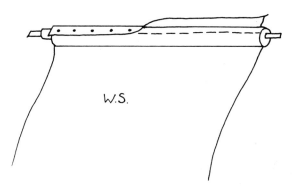

76 POSITIONING THE FABRIC ALONG THE GUIDE LINES PROVIDED

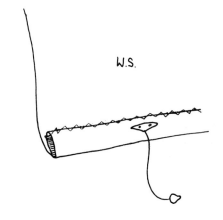

77 THE FINISHED BLIND WITH THE BATTEN IN ITS CASING, AND THE ACORN FITTING SCREWED IN

the blind with braid. Alternatively, cut a shaped edge in blind fabric and fix to the back of the casing with adhesive.

BOX CUSHIONS FOR BEDHEAD

Box cushions hung from curtain poles above beds or divans make comfortable and practical head or back rests. Their tailored appearance well suits a masculine bedroom or study.

Make the inner pad for these cushions from a rigid filling such as plastic or latex foam block. Have these cut to the size required (or cut them yourself using a very sharp knife). Cover with calico or other strong cotton fabric before making the outer cover. Openings for these covers need to be large enough to enable the rigid pad to be inserted easily, so make them to extend round the side edges 5-10 cm (2-4 in) or the depth of the welt. Position them at the lower edge of the cushion cover. When measuring and cutting out the fabric remember to take the exact measurements of the pad, for this is rigid. Add 1.3 cm (½ in) turnings all round (1.9 cm [¾ in] if the fabric frays easily).

Make box cushions to match or co-ordinate with bedcovers and valances, choosing closely woven fabrics that wash and wear well. This method of construction may also be used when making seat cushions for chairs.

To make up

1 Measure the pad carefully and prepare a cutting plan to estimate the amount of fabric required (*see example, Fig 78*). Cut out the fabric following your plan and allow 1.3 cm (½ in) turnings on all pieces. Centralize patterns where necessary. If the fabric frays easily, neaten all the raw edges before making up the cushion cover.

2 With right sides facing, tack the front and back sections together in the centre of the cover to hold the two pieces firmly in position whilst the welts are tacked in. Pin each welt to the cushion fabric separately, placing right sides together. Tack 2.5 cm (1 in) from the raw edge of the welt (*Fig 79*) to enable the piping cord and bias strips to be inserted between. Tack and machine the corner seams of the welt to within 1.3 cm (½ in) of each edge, taking 1.3 cm (½ in) turnings. Press the four corner seams open.

3 Prepare and cut the bias strips and the piping cord and apply it to the front and back sections of the cover, inserting it between the welt and the front and back sections. Pin and tack, clipping corners. Machine stitch round the front section using a zipper foot attachment and stitching as closely as possible to the piping cord. Do not machine the bottom section until the loops have been inserted.

4 For the loops cut a strip of fabric on the straight grain 15 cm (6 in) wide and long enough to hang round the curtain pole (approximately 28-38 cm [11-15 in]). Fold in half lengthwise with right sides facing. Pin and tack a 1.3 cm (½ in) seam and machine into position. Trim seam and neaten edges. Turn to the right sides and press in position, having the seam at the centre back (*Fig 80*).

5 Mark positions for the loops on the back section of the cover. Carefully unpick the tacking stitches at these points and pin and tack the loops into position on top of the piping cord, inserting the loop between the front and the back sections of the cover. Re-tack the seam.

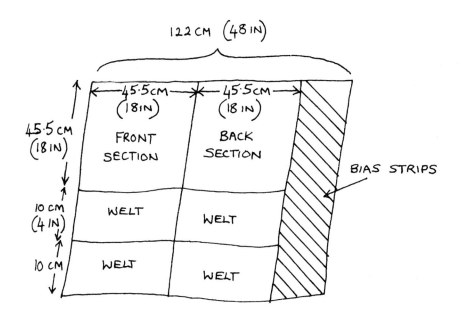

122 CM (48 IN)

45.5 CM (18 IN)

45.5 CM (18 IN)

45.5 CM (18 IN)

FRONT SECTION

BACK SECTION

BIAS STRIPS

10 CM (4 IN)

WELT

WELT

10 CM

WELT

WELT

78 CUTTING PLAN FOR A BOX CUSHION

W.S.

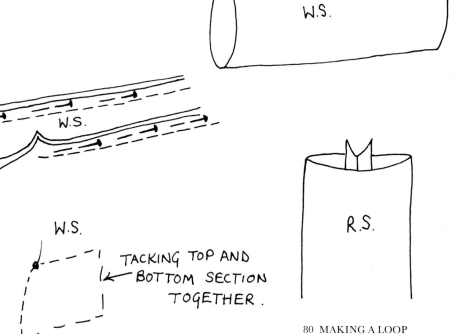

W.S.

W.S. (BEHIND)

W.S.

TACKING TOP AND BOTTOM SECTION TOGETHER.

R.S.

80 MAKING A LOOP

79 INSERTING A WELT ON A BOX CUSHION

6 Mark the position for the opening and machine stitch the seams of the back section, leaving the opening unstitched.

7 Remove all the tacking stitches and turn the cushion cover to the right side. Insert the pad and slipstitch the opening together.

TAILORED BEDCOVER

This bedspread is fitted to the size of the bed, with a pillow flap added that will fold over the top of the pillows. The wrong side of the flap is placed to the right side of the bedspread so that the fabric is reversed. This folds back over the top of the pillows so that the right side is uppermost. Make the pillow flap wide enough to allow it to overhang the ends of the pillows.

1 Measure the bed (*Fig 81*) and estimate the fabric requirements (*see p. 50*). Cut out the fabric for the central section, joining widths if necessary. Match patterns carefully using outside tacking (*Fig 11*).

2 Cut out the fabric for the frill, allowing 40.5 cm (16 in) for each inverted pleat at the foot and joining if necessary to obtain the required length. Position seams, if possible, so that they are hidden in the pleats. Make a 1.3 cm (½ in) double hem along the lower edge of the frill. Apply a trimming (optional) along the lower edge 5-7.5 cm (2-3 in) above the hem, making a guide line with tacking stitches first. Use small running stitches and matching thread and take care not to pull the stitches too tightly, otherwise the trimming will pucker.

3 Cut a piece of fabric for the pillow flap. This should measure the width of the bed (b) plus 35.5 cm (14 in) at each side of the central section, multiplied by the depth of the pillow (d).

4 Cut and prepare enough bias strips and piping cord to fit round the bed. Use the quick method described on p. 19, and pin

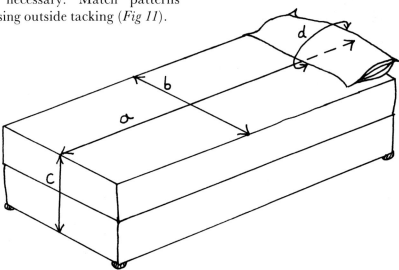

81 MEASURING FOR A TAILORED BEDCOVER
WITH A PILLOW FLAP

82

and tack the piping to the three sides of the central section. With right sides together pin and tack the frill over the piping cord (*Fig 82*), making an inverted pleat at each corner at the foot of the bedspread (*Fig 83*). Slash across the corners, trim the seams and neaten the raw edges.

5 At the top edge of the bedspread turn in a 1.3 cm (½ in) double hem and tack and machine stitch into position. Turn in a 1.3 cm (½ in) double hem all round the pillow flap. Tack and machine stitch into position. Place the wrong side of the pillow flap to the right side of the bedspread, centralizing it (*Fig 84*). Pin, tack and machine stitch into position.

For a fitted divan cover, follow the instructions for an ottoman cover on p. 124.

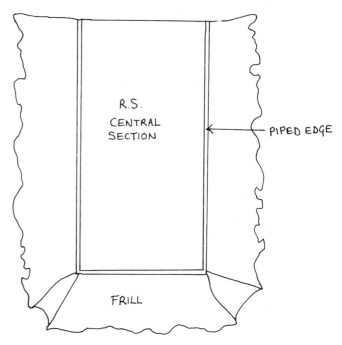

82 THE CENTRAL SECTION OF THE BEDCOVER WITH ITS PIPED EDGE AND FRILL

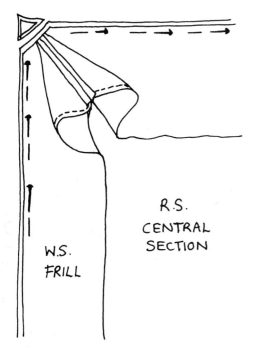

83 PINNING THE FRILL TO THE CENTRAL SECTION

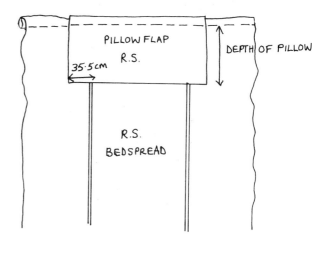

84 STITCHING THE WRONG SIDE OF THE PILLOW FLAP TO THE RIGHT SIDE OF THE BEDCOVER

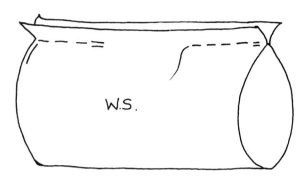

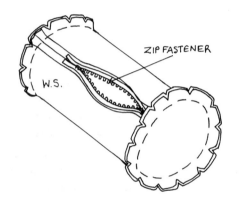

86 STITCHING THE CIRCULAR ENDS TO THE
TUBE AND CLIPPING THE SEAM ALLOWANCE

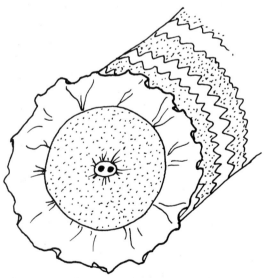

87 NEATENING THE CENTRE OF A GATHERED
END WITH A COVERED BUTTON

BOLSTER CUSHIONS

These long cushions are often used at the head of a bed or at the ends of sofas and divans. They are very decorative and can be made in combinations of fabrics with various edge finishes, buttons and trimmings. Avoid fabrics with large patterns as these may be difficult to match successfully at the seams.

Bolster cushion with piped seams

1 Cut two circles of fabric the size required, allowing 1.3 cm (½ in) turnings all round. Cut these using a paper pattern made using a large plate or tray.

2 Cut a rectangle of fabric on the straight grain, the circumference of the bolster pad plus 2.5 cm (1 in) for turnings and the required length of the cushion cover.

3 With right sides together pin, tack and machine at each end of the long sides of the rectangle, leaving an opening at the centre (*Fig 85*). The opening can be slipstitched together when the bolster pad has been inserted. Alternatively, use a touch and close fastening or insert a zip fastener in the opening, leaving equal hems on each side.

4 Prepare bias strip and piping cord (using the quick method on p. 19) and apply this to the two circular ends, clipping the bias strip to enable it to mould to the shape of the curve. (A frill could be made and applied as well as the piping.)

5 Pin and tack the circular ends to the tube with right sides together, snipping the seam allowance at regular intervals. Machine stitch using a zipper foot attachment, stitching as closely as possible to the piping cord (*Fig 86*). Neaten the raw edges and insert the

bolster pad. If not using a zip fastener, slipstitch the opening together firmly using matching thread.

A gathered end can be made for a bolster cushion by cutting a strip of fabric on the straight grain as long as the circumference of the circle plus 2.5 cm (1 in) and as wide as its radius. Join the short ends of the strip together and tack one long edge to the tube. Run a gathering stitch 1.3 cm (½ in) from the inner edge of the circle and draw up tightly to fit the centre of the circle. Fasten off ends securely. To neaten the centre sew a covered button over the raw edges at each end of the cushion cover (*Fig 87*).

To button down a cushion

Mark the centre of the cushion cover on both sides. Use double button thread and a long darning needle and secure the thread to the back of one button in the position marked. Take the thread through to the other side of the cushion cover to the point marked and then into the back of the second button. Take the thread back to the first button and pull tightly so that the buttons sink into the cover. Knot and fasten off securely (*Fig 88*). When buttoning a bolster cushion use an upholstery needle.

DUVET COVERS

Duvet covers are easily made from wide-width polyester/cotton or 100 per cent cotton sheeting or other easy-care fabrics. Choose wide-width fabrics where possible as these need fewer seams. Patchwork motifs or other appliqué can be used to decorate the duvet cover, or trim it using lace or frills. Make sure these will withstand frequent washing.

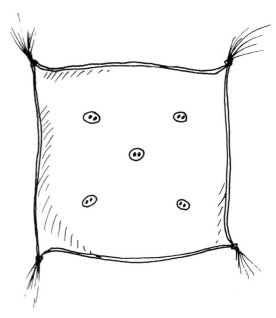

88 USE OF BUTTONING ON A SQUARE CUSHION

The cover should be made a little larger than the duvet so that it is not constricted in use. Make the opening along the lower edge so that it is away from the face and finish it with a touch and close fastening or press studs.

The amount of fabric required for the cover depends on the size of the duvet and these vary from single to super king size, so check measurements carefully before the fabric is cut out. For a single size 137 x 190.5 cm (54 x 75 in) allow approximately 3 m (3½ yd) of 228 cm (90 in) wide fabric. For a standard double size 205.5 x 198 cm (81 x 78 in) allow 4.5 m (5 yd) of fabric. As the covers are washed frequently make French seams where possible as these enclose all the raw edges and prevent fraying.

1 Cut out the fabric for the duvet cover in one of the following ways depending on the width of fabric available.

(*a*) Twice the length of the duvet plus

85

5 ATTRACTIVE USE OF STENCILS ON FABRICS AS
WELL AS HARD SURFACES

5 cm (2 in) x the width of the duvet plus 5 cm (2 in).

(b) Twice the width of the duvet plus 5 cm (2 in) x the length of the duvet plus 5 cm (2 in).

(c) Two separate pieces of fabric the length of the duvet plus 5 cm (2 in) x the width of the duvet plus 5 cm (2 in).

2 For methods (a) and (b) fold the fabric in half widthwise or lengthwise with wrong sides facing. Tack and machine the cover using French seams.

3 For method (c) pin and tack the two sections together with wrong sides facing and make French seams round the three sides.

4 At the opening at the lower edge of the duvet make a 1.3 cm (½ in) double hem and apply touch-and close fastening or press studs (*Fig 89*).

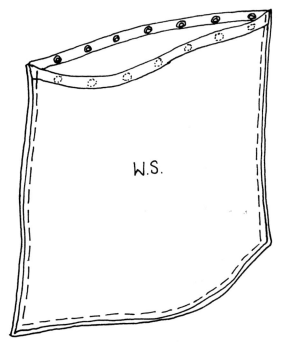

W.S.

89 APPLYING PRESS STUDS OR TOUCH AND CLOSE FASTENING TO THE OPENING

FITTED AND PLAIN SHEETS

Make plain and fitted sheets from wide-width sheeting in polyester/cotton or 100 per cent cotton, matching or co-ordinating them with other bed 'linen'. The size of the sheet is governed by the size of the mattress and these vary considerably both in depth as well as in width. Allow an extra 12.5 cm (5 in) all round the sheet for it to tuck under the mattress.

To estimate the amount of fabric required take the following measurements (*Fig 90*):

(a) The length of the mattress from the top to the bottom, including the depth of the mattress plus 25.5 cm (10 in) for tuck-unders.

(b) The width across the mattress, including the depth of the mattress, plus 25.5 cm (10 in) for tuck-unders.

For a plain rectangular sheet make 1.3 cm (½ in) double hems at the two side edges and the lower edge, but for the top edge turn under 1.3 cm (½ in) and then 5.0 cm (2 in). Tack and machine stitch into position. If there is a selvedge at the side or lower edge

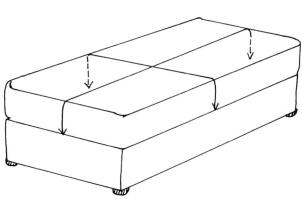

90 MEASURING THE BED FOR PLAIN AND FITTED SHEETS

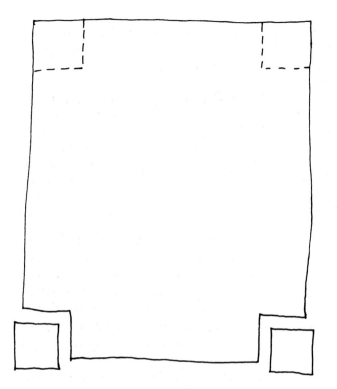

91 CUTTING OUT THE FABRIC FOR FITTED
SHEETS

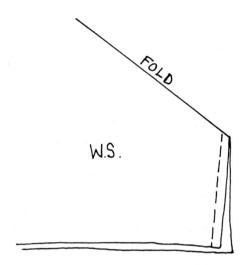

92 STITCHING THE CORNERS

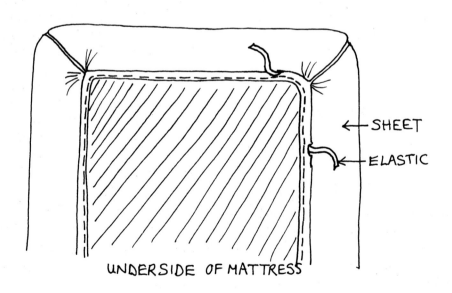

93 INSERTING ELASTIC TO GATHER UP EACH
CORNER

there is no need to make a hem. Decorative hemming stitching can be used at the top edge of the sheet, or rows of pintucking if a suitable machine and needles are available.

Fitted sheets

Estimate and cut out fabric as for the rectangular sheets but allow approximately 2.5 cm (1 in) less all round as the fitted corners will hold the sheet in place.

1 At the four corners cut out a square of fabric (*Fig 91*), the measurement being the depth of the mattress plus 10 cm (4 in). Cut the fabric at right angles to the edges. With right sides facing, join the two edges together, pinning and tacking a 1.3 cm (½ in) seam. Machine stitch into position and neaten the raw edges (*Fig 92*).

2 Pin and tack a 1.3 cm (½ in) double hem all round the edges of the sheet. Machine stitch into position, but leave 2.5 cm (1 in) of the hem unstitched 15 cm (6 in) from each corner seam. Insert a 25.5 cm (10 in) length of 1.3 cm (½ in) elastic through the hem at each corner, securing the elastic at each end and gathering up the corners (*Fig 93*).

PILLOWCASES

Make pillowcases in a plain or frilly style to match duvet covers or sheets. Decorate them with broderie Anglaise or other trimmings or make single or double frills in matching or co-ordinating fabric. Choose polyester/cotton or 100 per cent cotton sheeting as this is obtainable in wide widths, thus obviating the need for too many seams.

Pillows vary in size and can be square as well as rectangular, so measure them care-fully to estimate the amount of fabric needed. Make a pillowcase to fit loosely so that it does not constrict the pillow in use.

Plain pillowcase with flap – 51 x 76 cm (20 x 30 in)

A pillowcase may be made by folding one long strip of fabric or by using separate sections. The method chosen depends on the fabric available. Allow 1.3 cm (½ in) turnings.

1 Measure the pillow (remembering to be generous with the measurements). Allow an extra 18 cm (7 in) on the length for the flap. For example, for a pillow 51 x 76 cm (20 x 30 in), cut a piece of fabric 53.5 x 173 cm (21 x 68 in). Pin and tack a 1.3 cm (½ in) double hem along one short side. On the other short side fold over 6 mm (¼ in) to the wrong side and then 2.5 cm (1 in) to make a hem. Pin and tack. Machine both hems in position.

2 Fold the fabric (*Fig 94*), folding in the short side with the narrow hem for 15 cm (6 in) and having the right side of the pillowcase outside. Pin and tack the two long sides taking 1.3 cm (½ in) turnings, having the wrong sides together. Machine and trim the seams to 3 mm (⅛ in). Turn the pillowcase to the wrong side and complete the French seam (*Fig 95*). Turn the pillowcase and the flap to the right sides and press.

Alternatively, make the pillowcase using two sections if this works out more economically with the fabric available.

1 Cut out one section 53.5 x 96.5 cm (21 x 38 in) for the front section and one piece 51 x 81.5 cm (20 x 32 in) for the back section.

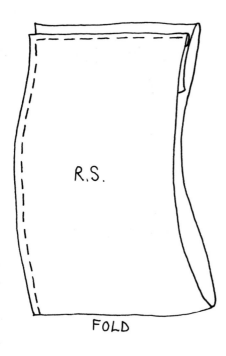

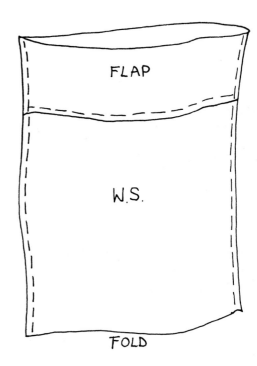

94 FOLDING THE FABRIC ENCLOSING THE FLAP

95 MAKING A FRENCH SEAM TO ENCLOSE THE RAW EDGE

2 Pin and tack a 2.5 cm (1 in) double hem along one short side of the front section. Machine. On the one short side of the back section tack and machine a 1.3 cm (½ in) double hem.

3 With wrong sides facing fold in the flap on the front section (*Fig 94*) and make a French seam round the three sides of the pillowcase.

Frilled pillowcase

1 For a pillow 51 x 76 cm (20 x 30 in), cut one piece of fabric 53.5 x 78.5 cm (21 x 31 in) for the front section, another piece 53.5 x 81.5 cm (21 x 32 in) for the back section and one piece 53.5 x 15 cm (21 x 6 in) for the flap. Pin, tack and machine stitch a 6 mm (¼ in) double hem along one long side of the flap section.

2 On the back section turn under 6 mm (¼ in) and then 3.8 cm (1½ in) to make a hem. Tack and machine stitch.

3 Make a gathered single or double frill following the instructions on p. 47. For a 5 cm (2 in) wide double frill cut strips of fabric 12.5 cm (5 in) wide on the straight grain – the length to be 1½-2 times the measurement round the pillow. Join the strips of fabric along the short edges with 1.3 cm (½ in) turnings to make a circle. Fold in half lengthwise and mark into four equal sections. Work two rows of gathering stitches in each section 6 mm (¼ in) from the raw edges (*Fig 96*).

4 Divide the front section into four equal parts and pin and tack the frill into position with right sides together. Distribute the gathers evenly allowing a little extra fullness as each corner (*Fig 97*).

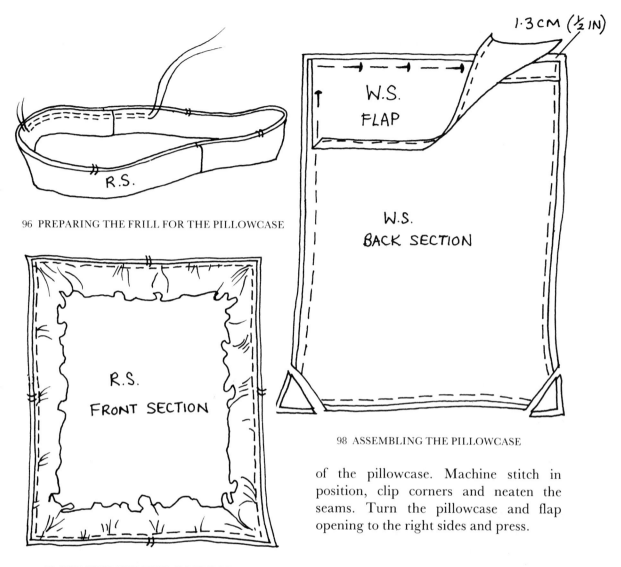

96 PREPARING THE FRILL FOR THE PILLOWCASE

97 APPLYING THE FRILL TO THE FRONT
SECTION, DISTRIBUTING THE GATHERS EVENLY

98 ASSEMBLING THE PILLOWCASE

of the pillowcase. Machine stitch in position, clip corners and neaten the seams. Turn the pillowcase and flap opening to the right sides and press.

CONE LAMPSHADE

When making cone, coolie or near-drum lampshades in firm fabrics use a strutted frame and make a pattern in paper first to ensure that the material fits exactly. Use the pattern to estimate fabric requirements.

Binding the frame (Fig 99)

Bind the frame using 1.3 cm (½ in) wide loosely-woven cotton tape. This provides a

5 Apply the back section to the front section with right sides facing, positioning the hem 1.3 cm (½ in) from the raw edges of the top section.

6 Apply the right side of the flap to the wrong side of the back section (*Fig 98*). Pin and tack round all four sides of the pillowcase, taking care not to stitch in the hem at the back section at the opening end

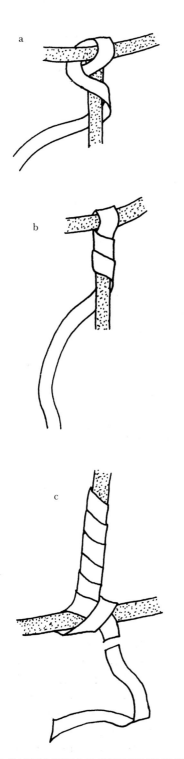

99 TAPING THE LAMPSHADE FRAME

firm foundation onto which to sew the material. For the struts allow approximately 1½ times their length and for the top and bottom rings allow twice the circumference. More is needed for the rings as the tape is bound round each joint of the strut and ring. Bind each strut separately and then bind the top and bottom rings. Always start and finish at a joint in the strut in order to prevent the tape from working loose.

With a plastic-coated frame it is not necessary to bind the struts with tape, but the top and bottom rings must be bound and also any struts where sewing or pinning will take place.

1 Place the tape under the ring, starting at the top of the frame. Tuck in and wind the tape round the strut, just overlapping it. Pull the tape slightly each time round as this stretches it and makes it mould more easily to the strut. Keep the tape smooth and taut and avoid any ridges that may threaten to appear.

2 At the bottom of the strut wind the tape round the bottom ring, taking it first to the left and then to the right of the ring (a figure of eight). Finish off with a knot and pull tightly. Trim off the end to the bottom ring.

3 Bind each strut in this way and then bind the top and bottom rings, making a figure of eight round each joint in the strut and ring. Finish off as before.

The cover

1 Make a pattern from which to cut out the fabric and estimate requirements. Take a large piece of stiff paper and place the taped frame onto it holding it firmly. Starting at the side strut draw along the outside of the strut with a pencil and mark

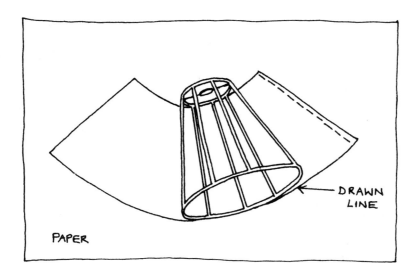

DRAWN LINE

PAPER

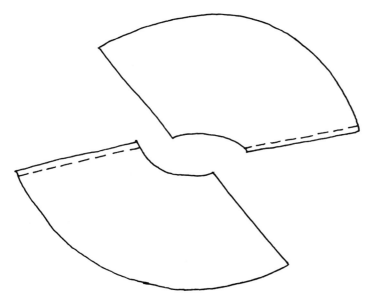

100 TAKING A PATTERN FOR A CONE LAMPSHADE

the top and bottom. Rotate the frame slowly, carefully marking along the top and bottom rings until the first strut is reached (*Fig 100*). Take care to hold the frame firmly or an accurate pattern will not be obtained. Make a 2.5 cm (1 in) seam allowance at one end.

Alternatively, for a large shade the pattern can be taken from one half of the frame only and the lampshade made with two pieces of material cut from the same pattern. In this case allow 1.3 cm (½ in) turnings on each section and remember to reverse the pattern on the fabric for the second half.

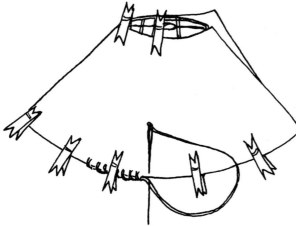

101 SECURING THE FABRIC TO THE FRAME WITH
CLIP-ON PEGS

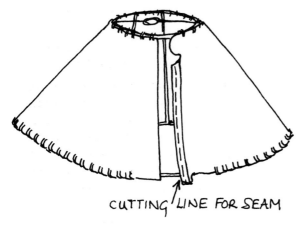

CUTTING LINE FOR SEAM

102 TRIMMING OFF THE FABRIC TO MAKE A
6 MM (¼ IN) SEAM

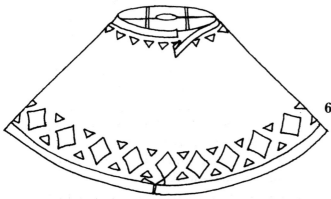

103 TURNING IN THE ENDS OF THE TRIMMING,
AND BUTTING TOGETHER. THE LAMPSHADE MAY
BE DECORATED WITH FABRIC PAINTS AND PRE-
CUT STENCIL DESIGNS

2 Cut out the pattern, fit onto the frame with clip-on pegs and adjust if necessary. From this paper pattern cut out the fabric and secure to the frame with clip-on pegs.

3 With double thread and a strong short needle sew through the fabric to the tape, stitching one half of the fabric to the top and bottom rings with blanket stitch (*Fig 101*). These stitches are covered by the trimming.

4 Stitch the other half of the fabric to the frame in the same way. Finish sewing 5 cm (2 in) from where the seam is to be positioned at each side of the shade. On the wrong side of the material and at each side of the shade mark a seam allowance of 6 mm (¼ in) using a ruler and pencil. Trim off the fabric to the pencil line, taking care to cut a straight edge (*Fig 102*). Overlap the seam and apply adhesive evenly to both edges. Press together firmly until the seam is secure. Complete the blanket stitching at both seams at the top and bottom rings.

5 Sewing trimmings to firm materials is impractical, so apply the trimming at the top and bottom of the shade with a quick-drying adhesive, starting at one of the side seams. Turn in the trimming 1.3 cm (½ in) and spread adhesive evenly and thinly to it with a small knife. Press firmly over the blanket stitches until secure. Turn in the ends of the trimming 1.3 cm (½ in) and butt them together.

6 If a plain fabric has been used for the lampshade it can be decorated effectively with fabric paints using a pre-cut stencil kit of a suitable design (*Fig 103*; see method of application on p. 77 concerning roller blinds). Take care to apply the stencil in the correct position on the shade using low-tack tape to hold it whilst the stencilling is worked.

EIGHT

Classic country house bedroom

•

INTERLINED CURTAINS WITH PINCH PLEATED HEADING

Interlined curtains have all the advantages of lined curtains and more. As well as helping the curtains to drape well, an interlining gives a luxurious padded look which shows off the texture and pattern of the fabric to the best advantage. Interlining such as bump or domette is placed between the curtain fabric and the lining sateen and is 'locked' into position. An interlined curtain also blocks out light as well as insulting against cold and draughts.

1 Cut out the curtain fabric and the lining sateen as for lined curtains (*p. 70*). Cut the interlining to the same measurement as the curtain fabric and join widths and half widths as necessary. As bump and domette are loosely-woven fabrics and tend to stretch, make the join with a lapped seam using two rows of zig zag machine stitching (*Fig 13*).

2 Place the curtain fabric onto a large surface with the wrong side uppermost. Lay the interlining onto the wrong side of the curtain, matching sides and lower edges. Fold back the interlining at the centre of the curtain and lockstitch into position as for lined curtains (*p. 70*), making two rows of locking stitches to every width of 122 cm (48 in) fabric.

3 Turn in 5 cm (2 in) at each side of the curtain and at the lower edge, folding both the interlining and the curtain fabric together. Mitre the two corners, cutting away a little of the interlining if the corner is too bulky. Tack and herringbone stitch the hems into position to make a firm edge (*Fig 104*). Slipstitch the mitred corners.

4 Place the lining sateen on top of the interlining fabric, right side up, and work rows of locking stitches as for lined curtains (*Fig 105*). Fold in the lining 3.8 cm (1½ in) at the side and lower edges of the curtain, matching mitres. Tack and slipstitch into position.

5 Work a row of tacking stitches across the curtain width 15-20.5 cm (6-8 in) from the top edge. This keeps the lining and the interlining firmly in position whilst the heading is worked.

6 Size up the curtains as on p.45 and find the correct position for the tape. If the heading is too bulky a little of the inter-

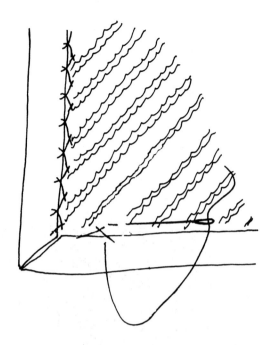

104 FOLDING THE INTERLINING AND CURTAIN FABRIC AND SEWING WITH HERRINGBONE STITCH

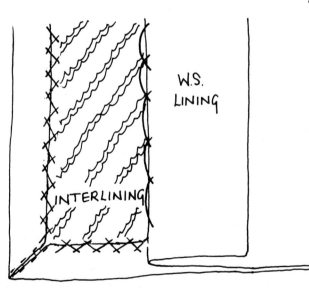

W.S.
LINING

INTERLINING

105 LOCKING THE LINING TO THE INTERLINING FABRIC

lining can be cut off to the required depth at the top of the curtain, but make sure that there is sufficient to catch it in the lower line of machine stitching which will be worked on the tape (*Fig 106*). For a standard pocketed tape follow the instructions on p. 45 and for a pencil pleated heading tape the instructions on p. 70).

7 Alternatively, apply a pinch pleated tape which produces deep triple pleats. This is approximately 14 cm (5½ in) in depth and balances well with long heavy curtains. Allow at least twice the width of the track when estimating fabric requirements. This pleating tape has two rows of suspension pockets for the hooks, which makes it suitable for use on most poles or tracks. It is appropriate for all weights of fabrics, including sheers and nets.

8 To apply the tape to the curtain, first cut the end of the tape in the centre of a group of pleats. Remember that there will be one left- and one right-hand curtain. Pull out the cords from the tape and knot each one. If there is an overlap arm at the centre of the curtain track, turn in 3.8 cm (1½ in) of tape and apply it to the edge of the curtain which will be at the centre of the track. However, if there is no overlap and the curtains are to butt together in the centre, turn in 9 cm (3½ in) of tape at this edge. At the other end of the tape pull out the cords ready for pleating up the curtain and turn in the tape 2.5 cm (1 in) and pin and tack it into position. Take care that the tape is applied the correct way up and that the hook pockets are facing.

Machine along the guide lines indicated, working both rows of stitching

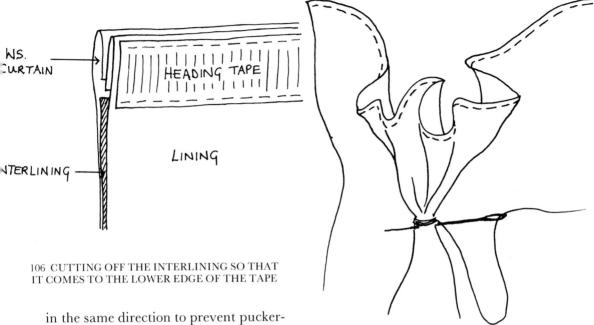

106 CUTTING OFF THE INTERLINING SO THAT
IT COMES TO THE LOWER EDGE OF THE TAPE

107 TACKING THE PLEATS AT THEIR BASE TO
SECURE IN POSITION

in the same direction to prevent puckering. Stitch along the side edges of the
tape, taking care not to machine over the
loose cords.

9 Pleat up the heading carefully, making
sure that the fabric does not pucker
between the pleats, and insert the
appropriate curtain hooks for the tape.
Tie the cords together and knot at the
side edge of the curtain. Do not cut off
the ends of the cord but tie them neatly
into a large bow or use a cord tidy. These
can then be released when the curtains
need to be dry-cleaned.

10 When using commercial tapes that draw
up pleats automatically the finished
appearance of the curtain can be
improved by using a few stitches to pinch
in the pleats at their base to secure them
firmly (*Fig 107*).

11 Once the curtains have been hung on the
track or pole they should be 'dressed'.
This means arranging the curtains into

even folds, 'breaking' the fabric between
each set of pleats forward from the track
so that it is proud of the pleats. Smooth
the fold evenly down the length of the
curtain and tie up with two or three
pieces of soft material. If possible, leave
the curtains tied for two or three days in
order to train the pleating.

Making a wadded edge

A luxurious edge can be given to interlined
curtains by padding the side and lower hems
with synthetic sheet wadding. It makes a
most attractive rolled edge. The curtains
must be dry-cleaned only and need careful
treatment.

1 When the interlining has been locked to
the curtain, but before the two sides and

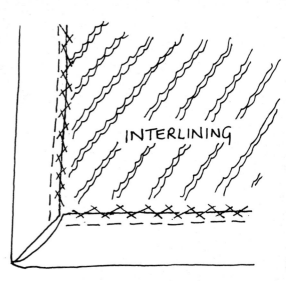

108 FOLDING THE WADDING INTO THREE, AND OVERSEWING TOGETHER

109 HERRINGBONE STITCHING THE WADDED EDGE IN POSITION

lower edge are turned over to make the hem, a 5-7.5 cm (2-3 in) border of wadding is applied to the wrong side of the curtain. In order to cover the wadding a 7.5-9 cm (3-3½ in) allowance must be made at the sides and lower edge of the curtain, and this must be allowed for at the bottom edge when cutting out the curtains. The wadding must then be prepared so that it fits into this allowance.

2 Make a line of tacking stitches down the sides and lower edge of the curtain to indicate the position of the fold of the hem.

3 Prepare the wadding by cutting strips 18 cm (7 in) wide by the length required; fold into three lengthwise and tack (*Fig 108*). Mitre the corners by cutting and butting them together and oversew them loosely to hold them in position.

4 Fold over the side and lower hems of both curtain and interlining to cover the strips of synthetic wadding. Mitre the corners

and tack, then herringbone stitch into position over the wadding (*Fig 109*).

5 Finish the curtains by applying and stitching the lining sateen as for the interlined curtains but turning it to leave a 5 cm (2 in) border all round.

6 Cut away the wadding at the top of the curtain to avoid extra bulk before applying the heading tape.

CURTAIN TIE-BACKS

Tie-backs are quick and easy to make, and as well as being practical they are very decorative. Use them to hold curtains back from the window to let in the maximum amount of light. Make them frilled or tailored, choosing from heavy or lightweight fabrics that match or contrast with the

6 BEAUTIFULLY STYLED CURTAINS FOR AN UNUSUAL SHAPED WINDOW

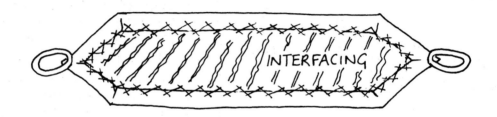

110 STITCHING THE FACE FABRIC TO THE
INTERFACING WITH HERRINGBONE STITCH

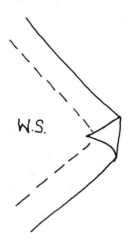

W.S.

111 MITRING THE POINT AT THE END OF THE
TIE-BACK

curtain fabric. Stiffen them with pelmet buckram or heavyweight non-woven interfacing and trim them with braids, piping cord, fringing etc. Make and hang the curtains before making the tie-backs.

Straight tie-back stiffened with interfacing

1 Decide on the length and width of the tie-back. To estimate the length tie a piece of string or a tape measure round the curtain to obtain the right effect. Take care not to make the tie-back too short as this could crease the curtain.

2 To this measurement cut a strip of fabric, interfacing and lining sateen to the length and width required. Add 1.3 cm (½ in) for turnings on the face fabric and the lining sateen, but cut the interfacing to the exact size of the finished tie-back. Cut the ends of the strips into points or curves.

3 Place the interfacing onto the wrong side of the face fabric. Turn over 1.3 cm (½ in) all round and herringbone stitch to the interfacing, mitring corners if necessary (*Figs 110 and 111*).

4 Sew a strong brass curtain ring to each end of the tie-back, using buttonhole stitch and a strong thread.

5 Place the wrong side of the lining sateen to the wrong side of the tie-back. Turn in the lining so that it finishes 6 mm (¼ in) from the edge of the tie-back. Slipstitch into position.

Shaped tie-back stiffened with buckram

1 Make a paper pattern of a shaped tie-back and experiment with different shapes before cutting out the fabrics. Fold and cut the pattern in half and use one side only to cut out the buckram shape.

2 Place the paper pattern to the fold of the face fabric and cut round the pattern, allowing 2.5 cm (1 in) turnings all round.

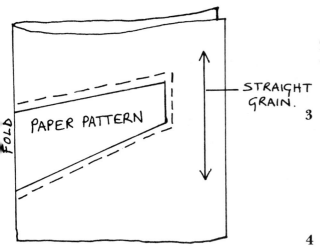

STRAIGHT
GRAIN.

FOLD

PAPER PATTERN

112 CUTTING OUT THE FACE FABRIC, ALLOWING
2.5 CM (1 IN) ALL ROUND

Cut a piece of interlining (bump or domette) and a piece of lining sateen in the same way, but allow 1.3 cm (½ in) turnings all round (*Fig 112*).

3 Place the buckram shape onto the interlining and dampen the edges all round using a small cloth. Fold over the interlining and press firmly onto the buckram using a hot iron. Slash curves and cut away surplus fabric at corners if necessary (*Fig 113*).

4 Lay the interlining face down onto the wrong side of the face fabric. Fold over the raw edge of the fabric to the wrong side of

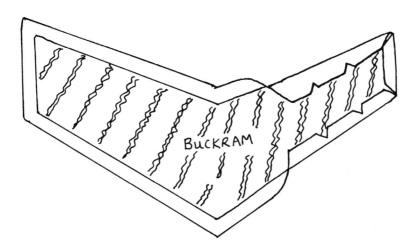

BUCKRAM

113 APPLYING THE INTERLINING FABRIC TO THE
BUCKRAM SHAPE

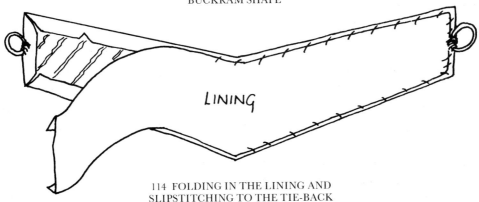

LINING

114 FOLDING IN THE LINING AND
SLIPSTITCHING TO THE TIE-BACK

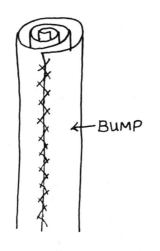

115 MAKING A FOUNDATION WITH A STRIP OF BUMP

the tie-back. Dampen the buckram and press the fabric onto it using a hot iron. Slash curves and mitre corners where necessary.

5 Sew on strong curtain rings at each end of the tie-back, using buttonhole stitch and strong thread. Place the wrong side of the lining to the wrong side of the tie-back and fold in 1.3 cm (½ in) all round. Clip curves where necessary and slipstitch into position (*Fig 114*).

Plaited tie-back

Make plaited tie-backs from three different fabrics that match or co-ordinate with the curtain fabric. To make the foundation use a strip of bump 20.5-25.5 cm (8-10 in) wide

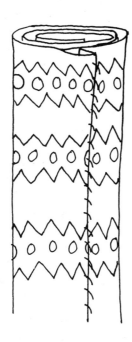

116 COVERING EACH ROLL OF BUMP WITH THE FACE FABRIC

117 PLAITING THE ROLLS TO THE LENGTH REQUIRED

and approximately twice the length of the finished tie-back measurement. Roll the bump as in (*Fig 115*) and herringbone stitch to hold in place.

Cover the roll with a 10 cm (4 in) strip of fabric the same length as the bump. Fold under one raw edge to make a 6 mm (¼ in) hem and slipstitch into position (*Fig 116*). Pin and tack the three different fabric rolls together at one end and plait them to the length required.

Trim off and bind the two ends of the tie-back with a 3.8 cm (1½ in) strip of fabric cut on the straight grain. Cut this the width of the end of the tie-back plus 2.5 cm (1 in) for turnings. Apply the strip to the tie-back as for a binding and turn in each end 1.3 cm (½ in) to finish. Slipstitch together and sew on a strong brass curtain ring with blanket stitching (*Fig 117*).

GATHERED VALANCE

A valance is a piece of gathered or pleated fabric which is decorative as well as practical. Valances are soft and informal in style and well-suited to the country look of today. Make them gathered or pleated using one of the commercial heading tapes.

Estimate the amount of fabric required as for curtains (*p. 35*) (they are really shortened versions of these). The depth of the valance should be calculated in the same way as for a stiffened pelmet, i.e. 3.8 cm (1½ in) of valance per 30.5 cm (12 in) of curtain drop.

Valances are not stiffened with buckram but they can be interlined with bump or a non-woven interfacing when thinner fabrics are used. Line them with a good-quality curtain lining sateen. Finish the back of the valance with a curtain heading tape and either hang it from a valance rail or attach it to a pelmet board in front of the curtain track.

Valances can be used round dressing tables and vanity units and are also effective when making bed canopies and drapes for tester and half tester beds.

Add a strip of contrasting or co-ordinating fabric 10-12.5 cm (4-5 in) wide to the lower edge of the valance to give extra interest. If the lower edge is not curved this can be cut on the straight grain. Glazed chintz in plain colours makes an effective edge.

1 Decide on the depth of the valance and allow 3.8 cm (1½ in) for the lower hems, 5 cm (2 in) for the heading and 2.5 cm (1 in) at each side edge. A gathered valance needs plenty of fullness, so allow at least double the length of the valance rail or pelmet board, remembering to include the return at each end.

2 Cut out the fabric and the lining sateen and, if necessary, join widths together using 1.3 cm (½ in) seams, and press open.

3 Make up the valance as for a lined (or interlined) curtain. For a gathered valance pin and tack a length of standard pocketed curtain tape onto the back of the valance, 3.8-5 cm (1-1½ in) from the top edge (*Fig 118*). Alternatively, use a pencil pleated or pinch pleated heading, taking care to arrange the heading tape so that when drawn up the sets of pleats are correctly positioned on the right side of the valance.

4 Insert curtain hooks in the heading tape and attach the valance to the rail in front of the track, or when using a pelmet board place screw-in eyelet rings to the board to match up with the hooks in the heading

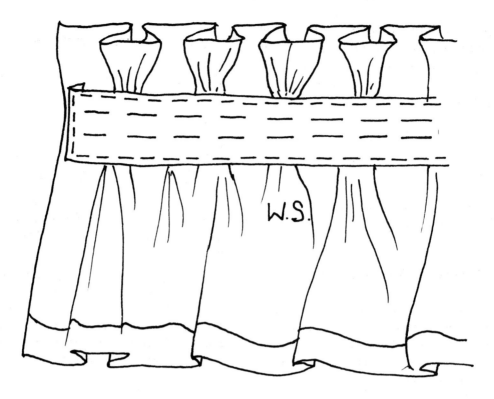

118 APPLYING CURTAIN HEADING TAPE TO THE
WRONG SIDE OF THE VALANCE

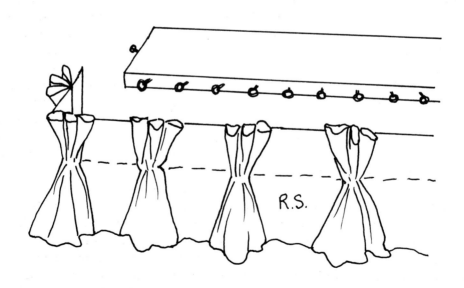

119 ATTACHING A VALANCE TO THE BOARD

tape. Hook the valance to the pelmet board using the rings (*Fig 119*).

5 Alternatively, if the heading allows, apply the valance to the pelmet board with a touch and close fastening. Use the 'stick and sew' type, applying the adhesive side to the board and sewing the matching side to the top edge of the valance over the heading tape. (For extra strength secure the tape further by stapling it to the pelmet board using a staple gun every 12.5-15 cm [5-6 in] along its length.)

BED DRAPES AND CANOPIES

Traditional tester and half tester beds can be draped using the instructions for lined and unlined curtains on pp. 70 and 44.

Elegant four-poster beds may be made from wooden kits bought ready to assemble. They can also be made using standard curtain poles and ring fittings. Screw the upright poles into the base of the bed to hold them firmly into position, and fix the cross poles with brackets for added strength. Alternatively, use the special rods, brackets and supports available from some curtain track manufacturers. A more permanent fitting for a four-poster bed can be made by screwing wooden battens to the ceiling onto which a hardboard facing may be attached. A curtain track can then be fixed to the battens and a frilly valance or stiffened pelmet attached with a touch and close fastening.

Select lightweight fabrics such as voiles, sheers and lace, or choose polyester/cotton sheeting to match the bedlinen, or light furnishing cottons that wash well.

For a lined curtain with a frill turn in the same amount of fabric for both face fabric

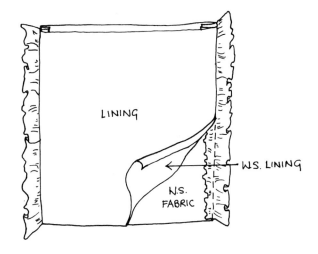

120 SANDWICHING THE FRILL BETWEEN THE FACE FABRIC AND THE LINING

and lining and sandwich the frill between the two (*Fig 120*) so that the view from the bed is as neat as it is from the outside.

Bed canopies

A small canopy can be made at the head of the bed by fixing wooden battens to the ceiling or walls and then attaching a valance rod to it. Make and attach the canopy in exactly the same way as a valance (*p. 103*). Position the battens so that they extend approximately 10 cm (4 in) at each side of the bed and extend them out from the wall approximately 15-23 cm (6-9 in). A straight curtain may be used at the back of the bed, being fixed to the same batten as the valance rod.

A 'coronet' is another attractive way of treating a bed and is easily made by using a flexible track fixed to battens on the wall. A decorative curtain rod may be fixed at right angles to the wall over the centre of the bed. The curtains can be hung from the pole and held back at the sides of the bed with

7 ELEGANT NET CANOPY OVER FRILLED
PILLOWCASES AND DUVET COVER

121 USING A READY-MADE CORONET COMPLETE
WITH FITTING

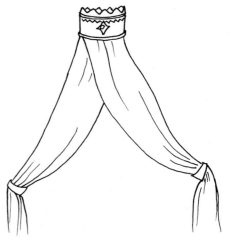

decorative or metal tie-backs. Alternatively,
a metal ready-made coronet complete with
fittings can be obtained from some department stores and metalwork shops (Fig 121).
This is fixed to the wall and the curtains
suspended from it and held back by tie-backs
or metal hooks. A third curtain hangs
against the wall.

LOOSE COVER FOR A HEADBOARD

A headboard looks effective when covered with a loose cover in a plain or quilted fabric, fixed under the bottom of the headboard with ties. This is an inexpensive and attractive method of treating wooden or plastic upholstered headboards.

Choose furnishing fabrics that match or co-ordinate with bedcovers and curtains, or use ready-quilted washable fabric or polester/cotton sheeting for easy-care covers. To quilt the fabric follow the instructions on p. 51, using a thin layer of synthetic sheet wadding between two pieces of fabric.

Quilted loose cover for a headboard

1 Cut out a paper pattern to the size of the headboard to estimate the amount of fabric required. (For a single size head-board 91.5 cm [36 in] wide by 61 cm [24 in] deep, allow 2 m (yd) of 122 cm (48 in) wide fabric.)

2 Quilt a piece of fabric to the size of the pattern plus 2.5 cm (1 in) turnings for the front section, using a piece of unbleached calico for the backing. Work this by hand or machine (p. 51). Remember that the fabric will be slightly reduced in size by the quilting process. For the back section cut a piece of fabric to the same size. Place the two sections together and notch round at intervals.

3 If the headboard is more than 3.8 cm (1½ in) thick it is best to insert a narrow gusset between the front and back sections. Piping may be used on the seams to give a tailored finish. For the gusset cut a piece of fabric on the straight grain long enough to insert round the two sides and

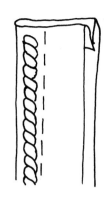

122 TURNING IN THE ENDS OF THE BIAS STRIP TO NEATEN IT

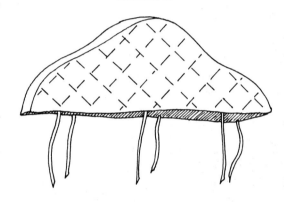

123 LOOSE COVER FOR A HEADBOARD

top of the cover. Cut and prepare bias strips twice this length to pipe round both sections (use the quick method on p. 19). Pin and tack this to the front and back sections, clipping curves. To neaten the ends pull out the piping cord for 1.3 cm (½ in) and turn in the bias strip (*Fig 122*).

4 With right sides facing pin and tack the gusset to both the front and the back sections, matching notches. Machine stitch into position using a zipper foot attachment. Trim seams and neaten the edges, clipping curves where necessary.

5 Turn up a 1.3 cm (½ in) double hem at the lower edges of the cover and tack and

machine stitch into position. Sew six 25.5 cm (10 in) lengths of white or matching tape in pairs to the back and front sections of the cover in three positions along the lower hems. Tie these underneath the headboard when the cover is in place (*Fig 123*).

DRESSING TABLE COVER

A draped dressing table makes an attractive feature in a feminine bedroom. Use a white wood kidney-shaped table, a small chest of drawers, a kneehole desk or use plain wooden shelves fixed to the wall. Fix a light plastic or flexible curtain track underneath the table top and curve it to the shape required. From this hang a pair of curtains which meet at the centre front and allow access to the storage space beneath. If possible, use a track with an overlap arm. Cover the top with a loose cover made from plain or quilted fabric adding a frill or small pelmet to complete the dressing table and cover the curtain headings. Protect the fabric on the top of the dressing table with a plate glass top cut to size. Suitable fabrics range from furnishing cottons to voiles and organdie.

Making the curtains

1 Curtains for this type of dressing table can be lined or unlined depending on the

124 COVERING A KIDNEY-SHAPED DRESSING TABLE

fabric chosen. Follow the instructions for making curtains on pp. 44 and 70.

2 For flimsy fabrics allow 2-3 times the length of the curtain track, or enough fullness to conceal the woodwork underneath. Lightwight furnishing cottons require 1½-2 times the width of the track.

3 Make the curtains to finish 1.3 cm (½ in) from the floor and if possible have an overlap arm at the centre front. Use a simple gathered heading tape at the top of the curtains as this will be covered by the frill or pelmet.

Covering the top

1 Make a paper pattern of the top of the table (draw round the plate glass top if there is one). From this cut one piece of non-woven interfacing. Cut out the fabric and the lining sateen using the paper pattern, cutting both 2.5 cm (1 in) larger all round to allow for turnings. Centralize any pattern where necessary.

2 Place the interfacing to the wrong side of the cover fabric and tack. Turn over the 2.5 cm (1 in) seam allowance to the wrong

side and herringbone stitch in position (*Fig 125*).

3 Apply the lining to the wrong side of the top cover, turning in 2.5 cm (1 in) all round. Slipstitch into position.

The fabric for the table top could be machine or hand quilted instead of interlined with non-woven interfacing, or it could be quilted matching fabric, if this is available. Use a thin layer of synthetic wadding and a piece of muslin or calico when quilting the face fabric; this gives an attractive padded effect to the top of the dressing table. Remember to allow a little extra fabric if quilting, as the fabric size will be reduced by the quilting process.

Making the pelmet or frill

1 Make the pelmet following the instructions given on p. 73 using heavy-weight non-woven interfacing as a foundation instead of pelmet buckram, as this is washable. Herringbone stitch in position. Pin the pelmet in position to the cover of the dressing table top and slipstitch neatly in place. This method of

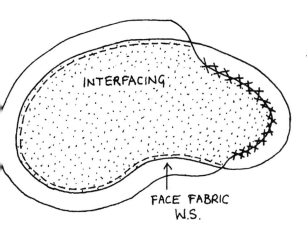

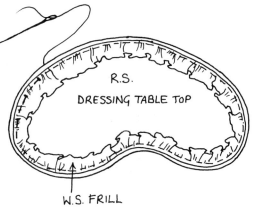

125 HERRINGBONE STITCHING THE FACE FABRIC
    TO THE INTERFACING

126 APPLYING THE FRILL TO THE QUILTED TOP

fixing prevents dust collecting at the top edge of the pelmet.

2 Alternatively, apply a gathered or pleated frill, or a wide lace edging to the dressing table top (*Fig 126*) following the instructions for a frilled cushion on p. 47. With right sides together pin and tack the frill to the top cover and machine stitch into position taking 1.3 cm (½ in) turnings. Clip curves and trim seams to complete the dressing table cover.

3 Do not make the pelmet or frill for a dressing table too deep, otherwise it will interfere with the smooth working of the drawers. A depth of 10-15 cm (4-6 in) is usually sufficient.

CLASSIC STYLE LAMPSHADE

This is one of the quickest and most satisfactory methods of making lampshades. It can be used for most straight-sided and curved styles of shade, provided the measurement round the narrowest part of the frame is not more than the top ring. Prepare the cover and lining from double fabric, pinning onto one side of the frame only. Stitch the cover to the frame first before inserting the balloon lining.

Choose fabrics with plenty of give such as silks and polyester crêpe-backed satins. (See chapter 4 for full details of fabric selection for this type of shade.) A rough estimate of the fabric required can be obtained by measuring the depth of the frame plus 10 cm (4 in) and the circumference of the bottom ring plus 12.5 cm (5 in). Cut the fabric in two pieces if necessary.

1 Tape the frame as described on p. 91. On a plastic-coated frame it is only necessary to tape the two side struts and the top and bottom rings (this is where pinning and sewing will take place).

2 Fold the cover fabric in half with the right sides together and pin to hold in position. Place this double fabric onto one side of the frame with the straight grain running down the middle (*Fig 127*).

3 Place a pin at ABC and D, pinning just into the top of the tape and not through to the back of the frame. Pin the fabric to the two side struts AC and BD, placing pins at 2.5 cm (1 in) intervals. Do not pin at the top and bottom rings until most of the fullness has been taken to the sides. Place pins on the side struts with the heads facing towards the centre of the shade. Pins on the top and bottom rings should face towards the centre, as this reduces the risk of damaging clothes and body.

4 Tighten the fabric at the top and bottom rings to remove wrinkles, pinning every 2.5 cm (1 in). Complete the pinning on the side structs, inserting pins first at 1.3 cm (½ in) intervals and then at 6 mm (¼ in) intervals.

5 With a hard pencil carefully draw a faint line over the pins on the side struts, extending the pencil mark 1.3 cm (½ in) round the top and bottom rings at ABC and D, and making a horizontal guide line (*128*). Tack through the double thickness of fabric approximately 1.3 cm (½ in) from the pins on the side struts to hold the fabric together.

6 Remove the pins from the fabric and machine down the pencil line from the top to the bottom using a medium-sized stitch and stretching the fabric slightly while stitching. This prevents the stitches from breaking when the cover is stretched over

110

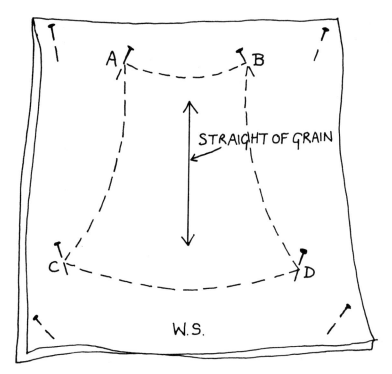

127 PLACING THE FOLDED FABRIC ONTO ONE
HALF OF THE FRAME

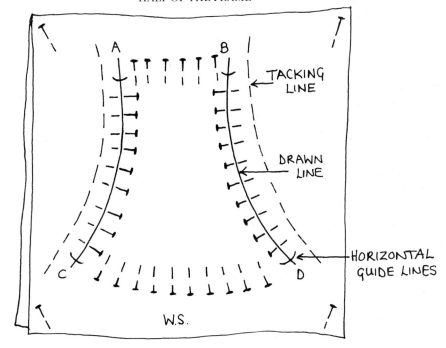

128 MARKING THE STITCHING LINE OVER THE
PINS ON THE SIDE STRUTS, AND TACKING THE
FABRIC TOGETHER

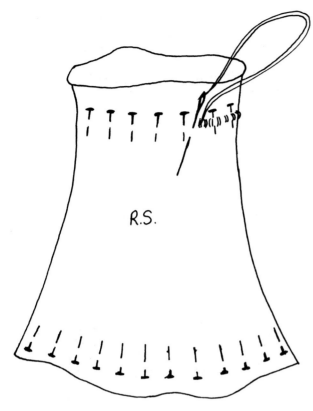

R.S.

129 OVERSEWING THE COVER TO THE FRAME
WITH DOUBLE THREAD

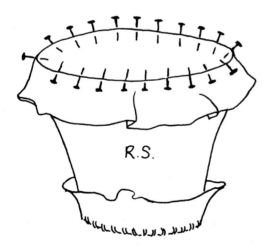

R.S.

130 PINNING AND STITCHING ON THE OUTER
EDGE OF THE RINGS

the top of the frame. Trim the seams to 6 mm (¼ in) at each side and cut along the fold line if there is one.

7 Prepare the lining fabric in the same way but stitch the seams 3 mm (⅛ in) inside the pencil lines. Press flat and set aside.

To fit the cover

1 Press the outer cover, keeping the fabric flat; do not press the seams open. Slip the cover fabric over the frame with the right sides outside, positioning the seams on the side struts. Match the horizontal pencil lines at the top and bottom rings. Pin the fabric to the frame, taking care that the seams do not slip out of place. Tighten and adjust the fabric so that it fits closely over the frame.

2 Oversew the cover to the frame using short lengths of double matching thread. The stitches should be sewn onto the outer edge of the top and bottom rings and worked from right to left (*Fig 129*).

3 Trim the surplus fabric from the top and bottom of the lampshade cutting as closely as possible to the stitching.

Inserting the lining

1 Drop the lining into the upturned shade matching seams and horizontal pencil marks at the top and bottom rings. Check that there are no frayed edges or loose threads on the inside of the cover before the lining is inserted. Pin the lining to the top and bottom rings, adjusting it by tightening the pins at both top and bottom until it is taut and smooth and all the fullness has been disposed of. To make the lining fit round the top ring unpick the seam down to the horizontal pencil mark

112

and spread out the fabric to enable it to fit neatly round the fitting; or, if necessary, carefully slash the fabric to make it fit.

2 Oversew the lining to the frame in the same way as for the outer cover. Position the stitches on the outer edge of the lampshade so that they are completely covered when the trimming is applied. Trim off close to the stitching.

3 To neaten the fitting at the top ring cut two pieces of lining fabric 10 cm (4 in) long by 2.5 cm (1 in), and fold each one into three to make two strips 1.3 cm (½ in) wide. Slip each strip under the fitting at the side of the frame; fold over to the outside, and pin into position (*Fig 131*). Oversew securely in place keeping the stitches well down on the stitching line on the outer edge of the shade. Trim off close to the stitching.

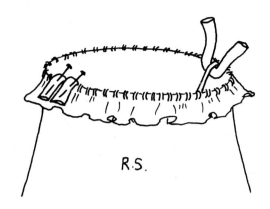

131 NEATENING THE FITTING WITH TWO STRIPS OF LINING FABRIC

Trimmings

Apply a trimming to the top and bottom rings to cover the stitching. Choose one that relates well to the fabric used for the outer cover of the lampshade. (See Chapter 4 for details on the selection and use of trimmings.)

1 Measure the circumference of the top and bottom rings to estimate the amount of trimming required. Add 5 cm (2 in) for turnings to each measurement.

2 To sew on the trimming, fold in the end 1.3 cm (½ in). Starting at a side strut, pin on the trimming and sew (*Fig 132*), using a zig zag type stitch, taking one stitch at the top and one at the bottom of the trimming. Take care that the stitching does not show on the inside of the shade. Finish by turning in the end of the

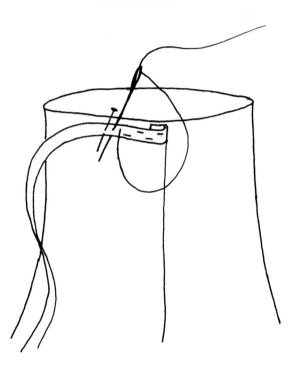

132 SECURING THE TRIMMING TO THE SHADE WITH A ZIG ZAG STITCH

trimming 1.3 cm (½ in) and butt the two ends together at the side strut. Make the two joins in the trimming on the same side of the shade.

ROMAN BLINDS

8 SMART ROMAN BLINDS GIVE A STREAMLINED LOOK

These blinds are very economical to make as they use less fabric than most other blinds and curtains. They rise up the window in soft folds and look well in both ultra modern and traditional settings.

Make Roman blinds from firmly-woven curtain fabrics and line them with curtain lining sateen. There is no need to stiffen the fabric. Use a special Roman blind tape to construct the blind.

Fix the blind to a wooden batten (approx-imately 5 x 2.5 cm [2 x 1 in]) at the top of the window. Attach the blind using a 'stick and sew' touch and close fastener. When the blind is pulled up it is secured on a cleat hook at one side of the window. A wooden lath is inserted into the lower edge of the blind to give it weight and make it work easily.

1 Decide where the blind is to hang – inside or outside the window recess. When hanging it outside add approx-imately 6.4-7.5 cm (2½-3 in) to the

measurement to ensure that the blind is wide enough to cover the window area. When making it to hang inside the window recess, make the finished width of the blind 2.5 cm (1 in) narrower than the window so that it fits inside easily.

2 Measure the window or recess. Cut out the fabric to this size and allow 18 cm (7 in) inclusive for turnings at the top and bottom hems and 7.5 cm (3 in) for the turnings at the sides.

3 Cut the lining sateen to the same size as the blind fabric and place wrong sides together. At the side edges turn in both thicknesses of fabric 6 mm (¼ in) and then 1.3 cm (½ in). Tack and press (*Fig 133*). Turn up the bottom hem 6 mm (¼ in) and then 10 cm (4 in). Press, but do not stitch.

4 Mark parallel guide lines down the blind from top to bottom for positioning the special Roman blind tape. (If the fabric allows, it can be folded concertina style and pressed gently to obtain straight vertical lines [*Fig 144*]). Make the side guide lines 1.3 cm (½ in) in from each edge. These should be equidistant and about 30.5-38 cm (12-15 in) apart, depending on how the fabric width divides (*Fig 134*).

5 Apply the Roman blind tape to the guide lines, making sure that each row of tape starts with a loop at the lower edge of the blind. Tuck the ends of the tape into the hem at the bottom edge and tack into position. Machine stitch along both sides of the tape through both lining and face fabric.

6 In order to make the blind fold easily up the window, sew horizontal lines of machine stitching across the blind to

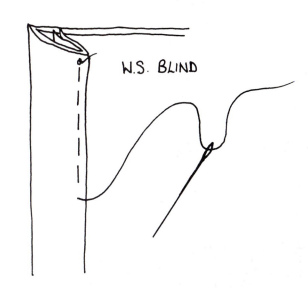

133 TACKING BOTH THICKNESSES OF FABRIC AT THE SIDE EDGE

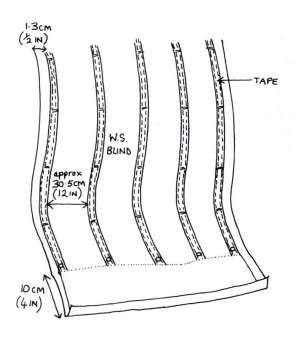

134 MARKING PARALLEL GUIDE LINES AND MACHINE STITCHING THE TAPE INTO POSITION

115

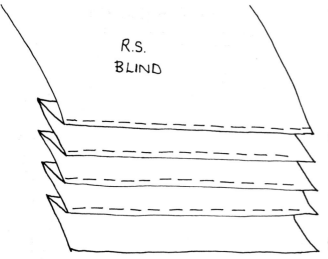

R.S.
BLIND

135 FOLDING THE BLIND WITH WS TOGETHER, AND WORKING HORIZONTAL MACHINE STITCHING ACROSS ITS WIDTH

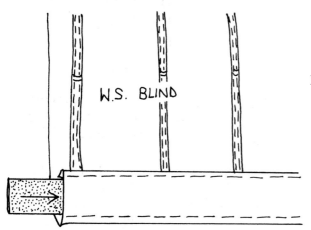

W.S. BLIND

136 MAKING A CASING FOR THE WOODEN LATH

correspond with every other loop on the tape. Start one loop up from the lower edge of the blind and, with the wrong sides facing, fold the blind across its width, using the loops as a guide. Pin and tack across the width of the blind on the right side of the fabric and machine stitch 3 mm (⅛ in) from the fold (*Fig 135*).

7 Tack and machine the lower hem into position, making a second row of machine stitching 3.2 cm (1¼ in) down from the first to make a casing for the wooden lath. Insert the lath into the casing and slipstitch both ends to enclose it (*Fig 136*).

8 With the wrong side of the fabric facing, turn over the top edge of the blind 1.3 cm (½ in) and press. Cut a length of touch and close fastening ('stick and sew' type) the width of the blind. Sew the smooth side to the top edge of the blind.

9 Apply the other side of the touch and close fastening to the top or the face of the batten. Position the brass screw eyes on the underside of the batten and in line with the vertical rows of tape on the blind. Fix the wooden batten at the top of the window. Mount a cleat hook at one side of the window.

10 Lay the blind flat and thread strong nylon cord through the loops on the tape. You will need double the length of the blind, plus the width, multiplied by the number of tapes you have used. Starting at the lower edge and on the side of the blind opposite to the cleat, take the cord up through every other loop on each length of tape and then across to the side of the blind, threading it through the screw eyes on the wooden batten and then down to the brass cleat. Knot all the cords together. Plait up the remaining cord and knot the end (*Fit 145*).

11 Hang the blind on the batten by pressing the touch and close fastening together. Draw the blind up the window and tie the cords round the cleat hook.

12 The blind can be decorated with a braid or other trimming and this should be

applied to the two sides and the lower edge. Use hand stitching to apply this and take care not to pull the threads too tightly otherwise the trimming will pucker.

SWAGS AND TAILS

Use swags and tails in tall elegant rooms where a formal window treatment is required. Although they can be varied slightly in style they look best in rich-looking fabrics and those that drape well. Decorate them with matching braids, fringes and tassels to complete the formal picture. Swags and tails are really draped pelmets which give the appearance of a piece of fabric thrown over a pole at the head of the curtains.

Swags and tails require a little practice and some patience to make successfully, so make a toile or pattern first in muslin or cheap cotton fabric to try out the design and size. This is essential as it gives practice and enables the right effect to be achieved.

The swag is the piece of fabric which is fixed along the whole length of the pelmet board. It should be cut on the cross grain of the fabric and is draped and pleated to a depth of one sixth of the curtain length (as with a stiffened pelmet or frilled valance). A series of swags may be made to fit across the pelmet board and these should overlap each other by 10-15 cm (4-6 in). Alternatively, one large swag can be made, but this is sometimes more difficult as it may be necessary to join fabric widths together.

Tails are fixed at each end of the pelmet board. They should be lined with a good quality lining sateen, chintz or other contrasting fabric and then pleated and

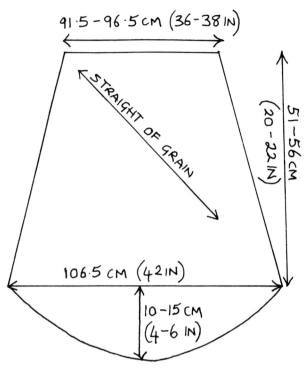

137 CUTTING PLAN FOR A SWAG

attached to the pelmet board. Make the tails approximately twice the length of the swag and cut them on the straight grain of the fabric.

Design the swags and tails as you would a pelmet, taking into account the position of the curtains when drawn back and the depth of the window. As the lining is an integral part of the tails and will be visible, choose a colour for this that matches or contrasts well with the face fabric. Variations of swags and tails can be made to suit individual windows but it is always advisable to make a toile or mock-up in cheap cotton first.

Making the swag

1 Cut out the swag on the cross grain of the fabric to ensure that a good drape is

9 FLOOR-LENGTH DOUBLE SWAG LACE
CURTAINS ADORNED WITH ROSETTES

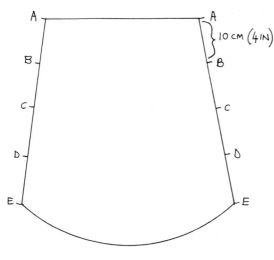

138 POSITIONS FOR PLEATING

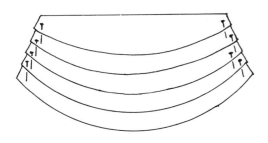

139 PLEATING THE SWAG

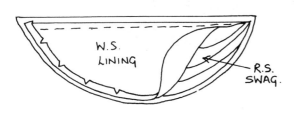

140 APPLYING THE LINING TO THE SWAG WITH
RS TOGETHER

achieved. Use Fig 137 as a guide to measurements and proportions. These apply to most swags and can be adjusted if necessary. Allow 1.3 cm (½ in) turnings all round. Fold in the turning allowance and press.

2 Mark out the positions for the pleating down each side of the swag, making the spaces approximately 10 cm (4 in) apart (*Fig 138*). Fold up the pleats, taking B to A, C to B, D to C and E to D (*Fig 139*). Pin and stitch the pleats into position when they have been draped satisfactorily.

3 Cut out the lining fabric to the size of the draped swag and allow 1.3 cm (½ in) turnings all round. Fold the turning allowance to the wrong side and press. With the right sides together pin and tack the top edge of the lining to the top edge of the swag and machine stitch into position (*Fig 140*). Turn the right sides out and slipstitch the lining to the curved edge of the swag.

4 Cut a length of touch and close fastening to the measurement of the top edge of the swag. Use the 'stick and sew' type, applying the adhesive side to the pelmet board. (For extra strength secure the tape further by stapling it to the board using a staple gun every 10-15 cm [4-6 in] along its length.) Pin and hand stitch the matching strip to the top edge of the swag (*Fig 141*).

Making the tails

1 Cut out a pair of tails in muslin or cheap cotton first in order to obtain a suitable pattern for the drape. Allow 1.3 cm (½ in) turnings all round. Use *Fig 142* as a guide. Make sure that the tails pair up and face the correct way.

2 AD is the depth of the tail at the side of the

119

window. AB is the return at the end of the pelmet board, usually about 10 cm (4 in). This is not pleated. CF is the narrowest part of the tail before pleating. EF can be a straight line or a curve, depending on the style chosen.

3 Cut out the lining fabric to the exact size of the tail, allowing 1.3 cm (½ in) turnings all round. With right sides facing, pin and tack the lining to the tail, leaving the top edge open. Machine stitch into position. Trim seams and clip curves and turn to the right side. Fold in the top edges and slipstitch.

4 Mark positions for even pleats along the top edge of the tail. Fold the pleats into a cascade and stitch into position (*Fig 143*). Apply a touch and close fastening to the back of the tail, as for the swag. Decorate the swags and tails with tassels, rosettes or braids which should be applied with hand stitching.

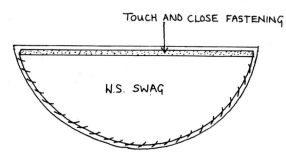

141 ATTACHING THE TOUCH AND CLOSE FASTENING TO THE BACK OF THE SWAG

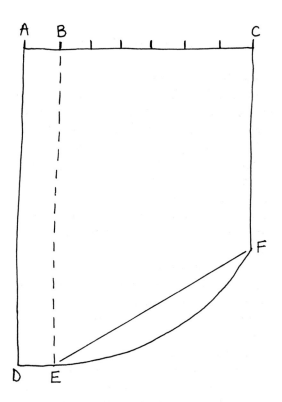

142 PLAN FOR A TAIL SHOWING POSITIONS FOR PLEATS

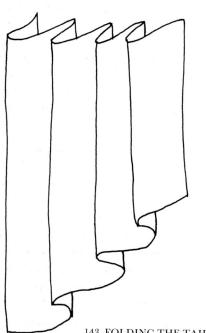

143 FOLDING THE TAIL INTO A CASCADE OF PLEATS

NINE

En suite bathroom

•

FESTOON BLIND

These blinds are similar in construction to Roman blinds but require more fabric as they are gathered both across the width and down the length of the blind. They are very ruffled and pretty and well-suited to bedrooms and bathrooms. As with Roman blinds they are fixed to a batten at the top of the window and drawn up by cords threaded through special festoon blind tape, which is attached to the back of the blind. They have pleated or gathered headings to draw up the fullness across the blind. Because they are so full and ruffled they are best made from lightweight fabrics that drape well. Lining is optional. When using patterned fabrics make sure that this lends itself to the scalloped style of the blind. Small random patterns do not present a problem. Decorate the side and lower edges of the blind with a gathered or pleated frill made in matching or contrasting fabric. For lightweight fabrics insert small weights in the lower hem of the blind at the bottom of each length of vertical tape; these help the blind to hang well.

1 Decide on the position for the blind and the wooden batten. This can be either inside or outside the window recess. Mount a curtain track onto a wooden batten 2.5 x 5 cm (1 x 2 in) or use a 'stick and sew' touch and close fastener to fix the blind to the batten. To give it extra strength, staple the rough side of the fastening to the batten at 7.5-10 cm (3-4 in) intervals using a staple gun.

2 Cut out the fabric for the blind, allowing twice the width of the track depending on the fullness required, and twice the depth of the window. Join widths of fabric where necessary, using a French seam for unlined blinds. If possible, position seams where the vertical tapes will be stitched so that they are as unobtrusive as possible.

3 To make a frill for the lower and side edges of the blind, cut a strip of fabric 10 cm (4 in) deep and 1½-2 times the measurement round the blind edges. Make a 6 mm (¼ in) double hem along one long side of the fabric and both the short sides. On the other long side make two rows of gathering stitches 6 mm (¼ in) apart. For ease of working divide into sections if necessary. Fold in 1.3 cm (½ in) double hems at sides and lower edges of the blind. Draw up the frill to fit

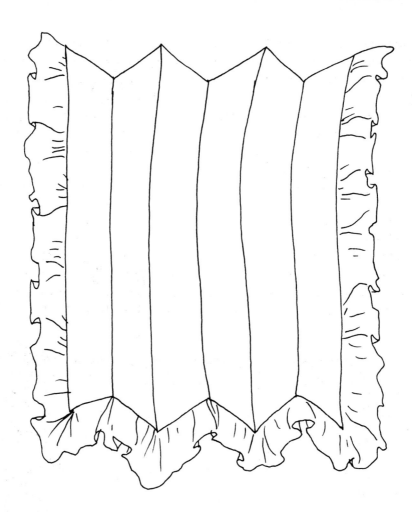

144 DECORATING THE SIDES AND LOWER HEM
WITH A GATHERED FRILL. FOLD THE BLIND
CONCERTINA STYLE TO OBTAIN GUIDE LINES
FOR THE TAPE

round the lower hem and side edges, and pin and tack to the wrong side of the blind; neaten raw edges if necessary. Machine stitch into position.

4 Apply a pencil pleated curtain heading tape to the top of the blind in the usual way, folding in the top edge of the blind 1.3 cm (½ in). Tack and machine stitch into position.

5 Mark the positions for the vertical tape, making guide lines equidistant and approximately 25.5-51 cm (10-20 in) apart, depending on the fabric pattern and the number of swags required. If the fabric allows, fold it concertina style and press to give straight guide lines (*Fig 144*). Pin and tack lengths of festoon tape down each side of the blind 2.5 cm (1 in) in from the frilled edge and down the marked vertical guide lines. Make sure that a loop in the tape is positioned approximately 3.8 cm (1½ in) from the lower edge of the blind. Knot the draw cords at the base of the blind and machine stitch into position using one row of stitching down the centre of the tape.

6 Draw up the heading tape at the top of the blind so that it fits the window width. Do not cut off the surplus cords but tie them round a cord tidy. Insert curtain hooks into the tape approximately every 7.5 cm (3 in) if using a track on the batten. Alternatively, if using a touch and close fastener, stitch the smooth side to the heading tape at the top of the blind.

7 Position screw eyes into the underside of the wooden batten at the top of the window so that they are in line with each length of vertical tape. Position a cleat hook at the side of the window.

8 To give extra strength at the lower edge of the blind insert a small curtain ring in the bottom loop on each length of vertical tape. Draw up the cords in the vertical tape from the top of the blind so that it fits the window length, and knot. Do not cut off the surplus cord, but tie it neatly.

9 Starting at the edge of the blind opposite to the cleat hook, thread up the blind with nylon cord in the same way as for the Roman blind (*p. 116*), first tying each length of cord to the ring at the lower edge of the blind and threading it through every other loop on the tape (*Fig 145*).

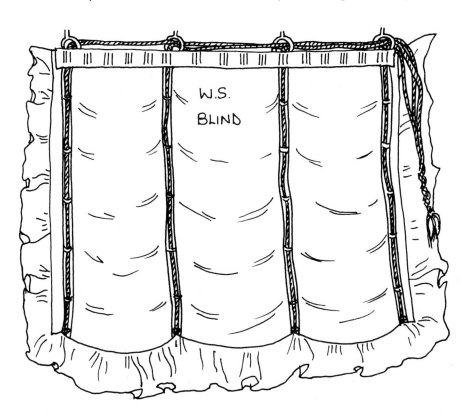

145 THE FESTOON BLIND WITH NYLON CORDS
THREADED THROUGH THE LOOPS AND PLAITED
AT THE SIDE

123

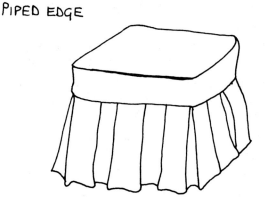

146 LOOSE COVER STYLES FOR OTTOMANS,
TRUNKS AND STOOLS

LOOSE COVER FOR OTTOMAN/STOOL/TRUNK

A simple loose cover for an ottoman or trunk can be made in the following way. It is a useful way of dressing up a utilitarian piece of furniture and matching it to other soft furnishings. Use a foam block cut to the size of the top to make extra seating units. A dressing table stool may also be covered using the same method.

Choose firmly-woven furnishing cottons that wash well and that are crease-resistant, and remember to pre-shrink the piping cord before use. (Boil it for five minutes and let it dry thoroughly.)

For a gathered frill allow 1½-2 times the measurement round the ottoman. For an inverted pleat at each corner allow 20.5 cm (8 in) extra for each 5 cm (2 in) pleat.

Ottoman cover with inverted corner pleats

1 Make a paper pattern of the top of the ottoman cover or stool and add 1.3 cm (½ in) for turnings. To estimate the amount of fabric needed take the necessary measurements and make a cutting plan (*Fig 147*). Ensure that the selvedge runs down the fabric from the top to the bottom of the ottoman on both the skirt and the welt sections.

2 Cut out the fabric allowing 1.3 cm (½ in) turnings on all sections. For a square or rectangular ottoman, trunk or stool, cut four welts of equal depth (usually 7.5-10 cm [3-4 in]) by the length of the sides, plus 1.3 cm (½ in) turnings. Join the four welt sections together along the short sides using 1.3 cm (½ in) turnings. Press

124

seams open (*Fig 148*). The seams on the corners give the cover extra strength and ensure a good fit.

3 Prepare and cut enough bias strips and piping cord to fit round the top and bottom of the welt. Apply this to the right side of the top section, snipping the corners and joining (*Fig 30*).

4 With right sides facing, apply the welt sections to the top section, matching the corners carefully. Tack and machine stitch into position. Apply the piping cord and bias strip to the lower edges of the welt sections in the same way and tack and machine stitch into position.

5 Prepare and cut out the four frill sections, matching patterns carefully, and join them as for the welt sections. Turn up a 1.3 cm (½ in) double hem at the lower edge and machine stitch into position.

6 Pin the frill to the piped edge of the welt with the right sides facing, having the seams at the corners. Make a 5 cm (2 in) inverted pleat at each corner and pin and tack into position (*Fig 149*). Machine stitch the frill using a zipper foot attachment and neaten the seams with a zig zag stitch.

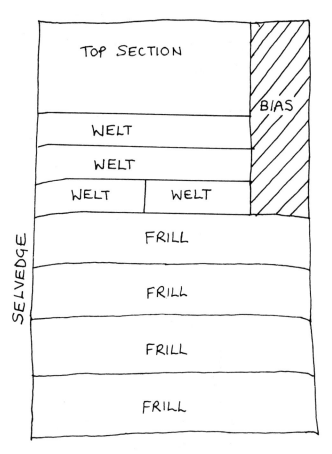

147 MAKING A CUTTING PLAN TO ESTIMATE FABRIC REQUIREMENTS FOR AN OTTOMAN COVER

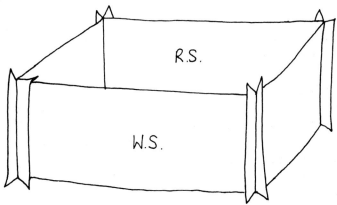

148 MAKING SEAMS AT THE CORNERS TO ENSURE A GOOD FIT

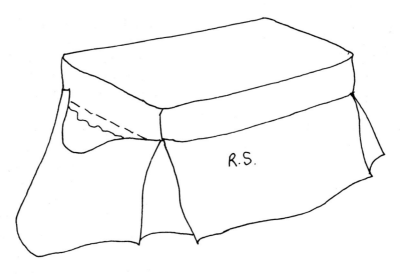

149 MAKING AN INVERTED PLEAT AT EACH
CORNER

SQUAB CUSHION WITH TIES

Make these cushions for small bedroom and
bathroom chairs, matching them to other
soft furnishings. For the bedroom choose
reasonably hard-wearing fabrics such as
furnishing cottons, linen union, corduroy or
other lightweight upholstery fabrics. For the
bathroom choose fabrics that wash well such
as towelling, printed furnishing cottons and
other firm fabrics that do not stretch easily.

Use plastic or latex foam sheets 1.3-2.5 cm
(½-1 in) thick to make the pad. Alternatively, buy a suitably-shaped pad from a
department store. To make a pad, cut out the
foam to the shape required, using scissors for
thin pieces and a sharp knife for thicker
sheets. Remember to cover the pad with a
cotton fabric or calico to protect it from wear.

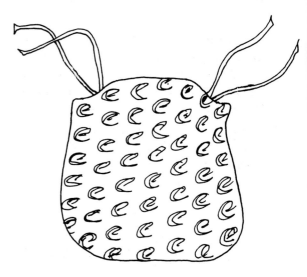

150 SHAPED SQUAB CUSHION WITH TIES

1 Make a paper pattern of the chair seat.
   Lay a piece of newspaper or brown paper
   on the seat and draw all round. Fold the
   pattern in half lengthwise to make sure
   that both sides are the same and that the
   pattern fits well. Check the fit of the
   pattern on the chair and adjust or trim as
   necessary. Mark the positions for the ties
   (*Fig 151*).

2 Cut out the foam shape using the paper
   pattern, drawing round it with a felt tip
   pen and marking the positions for the ties.
   For a cushion without a welt use foam
   approximately 2.5 cm (1 in) thick.

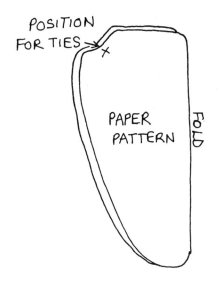

151 MAKING A PATTERN OF THE CHAIR SEAT

Tack the bias strip and the piping cord to the right side of the front section of the cover, tacking close to the cord. Clip curves where necessary. Machine stitch into position using a zipper foot attachment.

3 Cut out two pieces of fabric to the size of the paper pattern plus 2.5 cm (1 in) all round. This allows for the thickness of the foam and for 1.3 cm (½ in) turnings. Centralise any patterns or motifs.

4 Prepare and cut enough bias strip and piping cord to fit round the sides of the cushion, plus a little extra. Use the quick method of cutting described on p. 19.

5 To make the ties to hold the cushion to the chair, cut strips of fabric 3.2 cm (¼ in) wide on the straight grain and long enough to make two ties – 61 cm (24 in). Fold in half lengthwise and press. Turn in all edges 6 mm (¼ in) and press. Machine all round (*Fig 152*). Mark the positions for the ties. Fold these in half and apply to the front section of the cover, stitching firmly into position (*Fig 153*).

6 Pin and tack the top section to the bottom section of the cushion cover, leaving an opening across the back edge. Allow 20.5-25.5 cm (8-10 in) for this, depending on the size of the cushion, so that the pad can be inserted easily. Machine stitch into position, clip curves and neaten the raw edges. Insert the foam pad and slipstitch the opening together. Alternatively, bind the opening and apply a touch and close fastening.

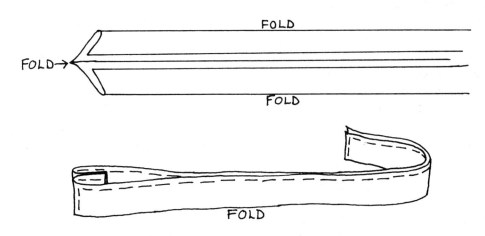

152 FOLDING THE FABRIC TO MAKE THE TIES

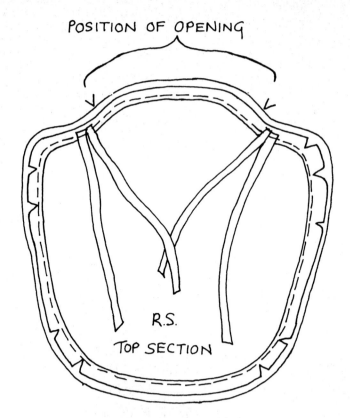

POSITION OF OPENING

R.S.

TOP SECTION

153 APPLYING THE TIES TO THE RIGHT SIDE OF
THE TOP SECTION

AUSTRIAN BLIND

Choose nets and sheer fabrics for making these blinds in bedrooms and bathrooms. Whilst allowing the maximum amount of light to filter through, they provide privacy and shade as well as obscuring unpleasant views. They are an ideal choice for bedrooms and bathrooms.

Be generous when estimating fabric requirements as sheer fabrics look their best when hanging in generous folds. Remember to stitch man-made fabrics with synthetic threads, and use binding tape and heading tapes in man-made fibres. Patterned curtain nets are sold by the metre or yard from a roll and can be bought in standard drops with ready-made headings and hems.

1 Cut out the fabric to twice the width of the window measurement and 30.5-35.5 cm (12-14 in) longer than its depth. At the side edges fold over a 1.3 cm (½ in) double hem. Tack and machine into position. Cut off the ready-made heading, if there is one, and turn over 19 cm (7½ in) at the top edge. Fold in 1.3 cm (½ in) and tack a 19 cm (7½ in) hem. Machine into position. To make a casing for a curtain pole, work another row of machine stitching approximately 10 cm (4 in) from the first (*Fig 154*).

2 Mark the positions for vertical tapes 25.5-38 cm (10-15 in) apart (*Fig 155*). Exclude the casing at the top edge of the blind. Tack synthetic standard curtain tape to the guide lines and the two side hems and

128

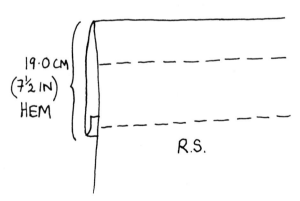

19.0 CM
(7½ IN)
HEM

R.S.

154 FOLDING OVER THE TOP EDGE TO MAKE A
CASING

machine stitch into position, knotting the
cords of the tape at the top. (Alternatively,
use special Austrian blind tape and cords
and follow the instgructions for a festoon
blind on p. 121.)

3 Use a decorative curtain pole to suspend
the blind, making sure that the finials
extend approximately 5 cm (2 in) at either
side of the window so that the blind covers
the window frame. Slide the blind onto the

129

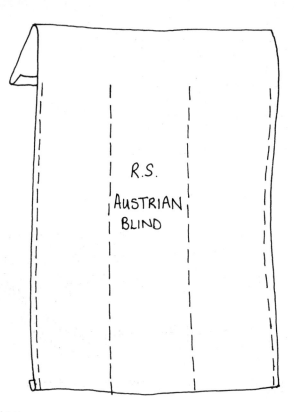

R.S.

AUSTRIAN BLIND

155 VERTICAL LINES SHOW POSITIONS FOR TAPES

pole through the casing at the top of the blind and gather it up to fit the pole. Draw up the cords in the vertical tapes to the required position for the blind, and knot firmly. Arrange the ruffles prettily (Fig 156).

TISSUE BOX COVERS

Tissue boxes look attractive when covered to match other accessories such as bath cushions, padded hangers etc. They also make delightful gifts. As the boxes vary slightly in size it is advisable to tailor the cover to a well-known make.

Choose polyester/cotton fabrics, dress or

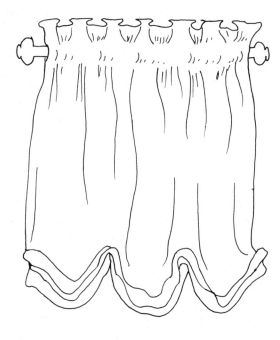

156 AUSTRIAN BLIND IN READY-TO-HANG NET

light furnishing cottons that fold well. Avoid those that are transparent, as they need a lining, or ones that fray easily, as they are difficult to handle.

Tissue box 38 x 25.5 cm (15 x 10 in)

1 Take the measurements of the tissue box (*Fig 157*) to estimate the amount of fabric needed. Cut a piece of fabric to this measurement plus 2.5 cm (1 in) for turning allowances, i.e. 40.5 x 28 cm (16 x 11 in).

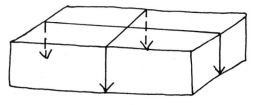

157 TAKING THE MEASUREMENTS OF THE TISSUE BOX

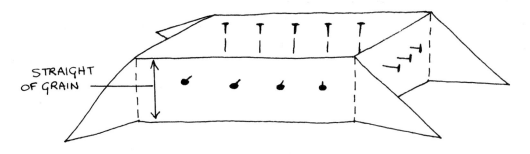

158 TACKING THE CORNERS OF THE BOX

2 Place the fabric right side down over the tissue box and anchor it in place with pins (*Fig 158*). Pin and tack the fabric at each corner, taking care to tack with the grain and at right angles to the top of the box. Remove from the box and machine stitch each corner. Trim the seams to 6 mm (¼ in). Turn up the lower edge, making a 1.3 cm (½ in) hem, and apply a trimming or frill over the hem using a small machine zig zag stitch.

3 Place the cover on the tissue box and mark the position for the opening with a tacking line (*Fig 159*). On a small box make the opening approximately 6.4-7.5 cm (2½-3 in) long, and on a larger one approximately 14-15 cm (5½-6 in) long.

4 Finish the opening as for a buttonhole and trim with lace or ribbons. Either make a machine buttonhole with a close zig zag stitch (suitable for firm fabrics only) or face the opening as for a bound buttonhole as follows:

(*a*) Cut a piece of fabric for the facing to the size of the top of the tissue box (11.5 x 24 cm [4½ x 9½ in]). Place this with right sides facing over the marked position for the opening. Mark this position through to the facing with tacking stitches. Machine stitch round the tacking line, keeping

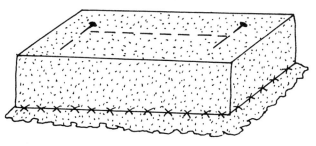

159 MARKING THE POSITION FOR THE OPENING

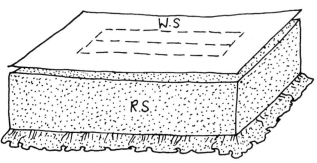

160 APPLYING THE FACING TO THE TOP OF THE BOX, AND MACHINING 1.3 CM (½ IN) FROM THE TACKING LINE

1.3 cm (½ in) away from it, and having right-angled corners (*Fig 160*).

(*b*) Cut along the tacking line with a sharp pair of scissors to within 1.3 cm (½ in) of each end, making diagonal cuts into each corner (*Fig 161*).

(*c*) Take all the facing material through the cut opening to the wrong side of

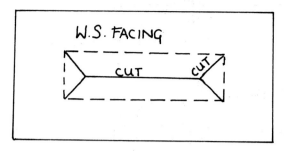

161 CUTTING THE FABRIC DIAGONALLY AT THE CORNERS

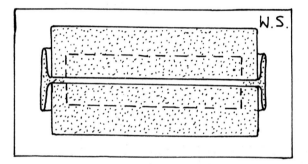

162 FOLDING THE FABRIC THROUGH TO THE WS TO MAKE AN INVERTED PLEAT

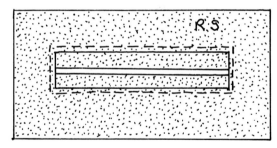

163 MACHINE STITCHING ROUND THE OPENING TO GIVE IT STRENGTH

the tissue box cover, and fold the fabric so that 1.3 cm (½ in) shows on the right side, forming an inverted pleat on the wrong side (*Fig 162*). Tack the facing into position and machine stitch the opening on the right side to give it strength (*Fig 163*).

Trim off the surplus fabric on the wrong side of the opening and neaten the edges with a zig zag machine stitch.

BATH CUSHION

A bath cushion adds a touch of luxury to a bathroom. Buy a ready-made bath cushion pad from a department store or chain store chemist, or make a pad to the size required using a waterproof plastic lining or shower curtain fabric to make the inner cover. Fill this with synthetic wadding.

For the cushion cover choose a quick-drying fabric such as shower curtain fabric, polyester/cotton, nylon or seersucker.

Make up the cushion following the instructions for a frilled square cushion on p. 47. At the top edge of the cushion cover insert two loops into the seam from which to hang the cushion. Make an opening on one side of the cushion and sew a touch and close fastening to the front and back sections (*Fig 164*). Insert the pad and suspend the cushion from two suction caps placed at the end of the bath.

SHOWER CURTAIN

These are constructed in the same way as unlined curtains (*p. 44*) but they do not require as much fullness. Shower curtains are usually fixed by hooks and rings from a pole or decorative rod or they hang from a special ceiling-mounted curtain track.

Use nylon showerproof fabric for making these curtains, or waterproof plastic fabric sold especially for the purpose. Alternatively, light cotton curtains may be lined with nylon showerproof fabric. This is

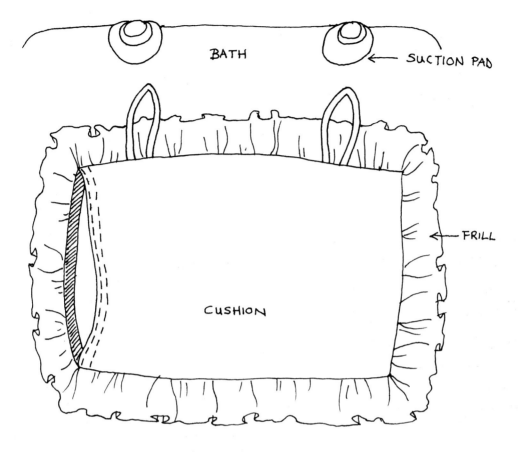

BATH

SUCTION PAD

FRILL

CUSHION

164 USE QUICK-DRYING FABRICS TO MAKE BATH
CUSHIONS

easier to sew than the waterproof plastic material.

When sewing plastic fabric use synthetic thread and a long loose stitch when machine stitching, and French seams for joining fabric widths together. Do not pin or tack the fabric as this would damage it; instead, hold the seams in place with sticky tape or paper clips. If the fabric is very shiny and does not slide easily beneath the presser foot, use tissue paper underneath the fabric to prevent it from sticking. Alternatively, spread a little talcum powder on the fabric to lubricate it through the machine.

Choose a synthetic heading tape for the curtain headings; alternatively, make holes

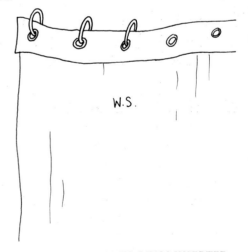

W.S.

165 PLASTIC SHOWER RINGS INSERTED
THROUGH EYELET HOLES MADE WITH A SPECIAL
PUNCH

in the fabric with a special eyelet punch and use special plastic shower rings or hooks for attaching them to the shower rail or decorative rod (*Fig 165*).

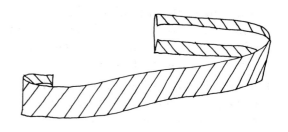

TOWEL TRIMS

Plain towels can be effectively trimmed using pieces of fabric that match curtains and cushions in bedrooms and bathrooms. Broderie Anglaise, lace or other trimmings that wash well and do not fray are also suitable. Choose ones that will not scratch or irritate the skin. Alternatively, personalize towels by trimming them with mono-grammed embroidery or simple appliqué. Use simple shapes for most effect and work on a machine with a swing needle and embroidery facilities.

1 To trim a towel with fabric cut four pieces 6.4-7.5 cm (2½-3 in) wide by the width of the towel plus 2.5 cm (1 in) for turnings.

2 Turn in each piece 1.3 cm (½ in) all round (*Fig 166*) and tack to each end of the towel on both sides. Machine stitch into position (*Fig 167*).

166 MAKING A FABRIC TRIMMING FOR A TOWEL

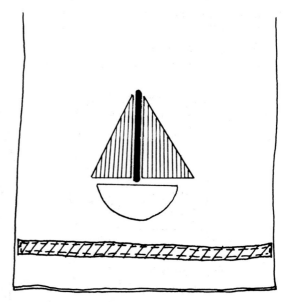

167 TRIMMING TOWELS WITH FABRIC AND APPLIQUÉ

BATH AND SHOWER CAP

Make these to match the bathroom scheme but chose polyester/cotton or fine lawn fabrics as these dry quickly. Use a waterproof fabric such as shower curtain material for the linings.

50 cm (18 in) of 91.5 cm (36 in) wide fabric makes two caps 45.5 cm (18 in) in diameter. You will need 50 cm (18 in) waterproof fabric; 153 cm (60 in) nylon lace trimming, and 75 cm (27 in) hat elastic.

1 Make a paper pattern of a circle 45.5 cm (18 in) in diameter. (The size can be varied by 5-7.5 cm [2-3 in] to make smaller or larger caps.) Using the pattern cut out a circle of both the cover and the lining fabric (*Fig 169*).

2 Place the shower fabric to the wrong side of the cover fabric and tack together round the outer edges. Tack the trimming to the right side of the cover fabric close to the edge, making sure that both the lining and the face fabric are enclosed. Overlap the

two ends of the trimming. Machine this into position using a small close zig zag stitch. Cut away the surplus fabrics as close as possible to the lace.

3 Make a casing for the elastic by making a tacking line 1.3 cm (½ in) from the outer edge. Machine along this line. Work another row of machine stitching 6 mm (¼ in) from the first line. Make a small hole in the casing in the lining fabric only (*Fig 170*), and thread the hat elastic through using a small safety pin. Draw up the elastic to fit and knot to secure it.

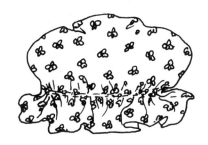

168 A BATH/SHOWER CAP

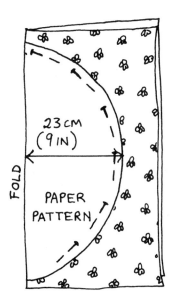

169 CUTTING OUT THE FABRIC AND THE LINING
USING A PAPER PATTERN

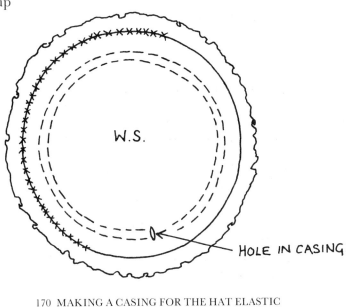

170 MAKING A CASING FOR THE HAT ELASTIC

Suppliers and useful addresses

•

John Lewis
Oxford Street
London W1 and branches

Furnishing fabrics, shower curtain fabric; roller blind kits and fabrics. Poly/cotton sheeting. Curtain track, poles, fittings and accessories. Interlinings, interfacing, buckram.

Laura Ashley
183 Sloane Street
London W1 and branches

Fabrics and trimmings. Chipboard tables. Lamps. Curtain accessories.

Sanderson & Son Ltd
Berners Street
London W1

Fabrics

McCullach & Wallis Ltd
25-36 New Bond St
London W1

Haberdashery, linings and interlinings

Habitat

Roller blind kits, furnishing fabrics

Kirsch (Antiference) Ltd
Bicester Road
Aylesbury, Bucks

Curtain tracks and fittings for curtains, bed canopies etc.

Rufflette Ltd
Sharston Rd
Wythenshawe
Manchester

Tracks and fittings for curtains

Paperchase
Tottenham Court Road
London W1

Stencil designs, brushes and paints

Limericks
Westcliffe on sea
Essex

Sheeting, ticking, curtain lining, pillows etc

Next Interiors
160 Regent St
London W1 and branches

Fabrics

The Colefax and Fowler Chintz Shop
39 Brook St
London W1

Fabrics, trimmings

Distinctive Trimmings
17 Church Street
London W8

Trimmings and accessories for curtains and blinds

Stencil Decor
Write to:
Eurostudio Ltd
Unit 4, Southdown Industrial Estate
Southdown Rd
Harpenden, Herts, for nearest stockist

Pre-cut stencils, paint in crayon form, brushes etc.

Carolyn Warrender Stencil Designs
91-93 Lower Sloane Street
London SW1

Stencil designs, paints, brushes etc.

Glossary

•

BRITISH TERMS AND THEIR AMERICAN COUNTERPARTS

appliqué – pieces of fabric or felt applied to another fabric

broderie Anglaise – cotton or cotton-polyester fabric with cut-out embroidery designs

buckram – a coarse fabric of cotton or linen that can be used for stiffening pelmets and curtain tie-backs

bump – coarse fabric or matting used for interlining

calico – unbleached muslin

crossway strip – bias strip – a strip of fabric cut across the weft and the warp of the fabric

cushions – all decorative pillows other than bed pillows

domette – baize or coarse flannel in which the warp is cotton and the filling woollen; used for interlining

duvet – bed covering used in Northern Europe that takes the place of both top sheet and blanket

heading – top edge of a curtain from which the curtain is hung

lining sateen – closely-woven cotton fabric with a shiny surface used for lining curtains

loose cover – slip cover

metre stick – yardstick

pelmet – fixture at the head of the curtains

roller blinds – window shades

selvedge – the edges of a woven fabric running parallel to the warp

squab – a loose cushion which is tied to a stool or a chair seat

tacking cotton – basting thread

template – a pattern used as a guide when cutting out

turnings – seam allowance

valance – pleated or gathered piece of fabric used at the top of a curtain; can also be used to describe fabric fitted under the mattress to conceal the base of the bed

wadding – batting or filling

zipper foot – a half foot which is attached to the sewing machine to facilitate stitching close to the zipper or piping; the design of the foot varies with the make of machine

Bibliography

·

Batsford Book of Lampshades Angela Fishburn (Batsford)

Batsford Book of Soft Furnishings Angela Fishburn (Batsford)

Curtains & Window Treatments Angela Fishburn (Batsford)

Textiles: Properties and Behaviour Edward Miller (Batsford)

Creating your own Soft Furnishings Angela Fishburn (Marks and Spencer/Orbis)

Quilting Averil Colby (Batsford)

Quilting: Technique, Design & Application Eirian Short (Batsford)

Traditional British Quilts Dorothy Osler (Batsford)

Style and Design David Hicks (Viking)

Stencilling: A Design and Source Book (Hamish Hamilton)

Paintability Jocasta Innes (Weidenfeld and Nicolson/ Channel 4)

VELCRO.

Rings $\frac{1}{2}$ WIDTH

CAWES APPROX 12". FROM
TOP.
6" AT HEM.

Index

•

Austrian blinds 128-30

Backstitch 8
Bases for lampshades 40-1
Bath cap 134-5
Bath cushion 132-3
Bed canopies 105-6
Bed drapes 105-6
Bedspreads 50-3, 82-3
Bed valance 53-7
Bias strips 17-19
Binding the lampshade frame 42, 91-2
Blinds 30-2, 77-80, 114-17, 121-3, 128-30
Bolster cushion 84-5
Bound buttonhole technique 131
Bound edge 17
Box cushion 80
Buckram 27
Bump 27
Buttoning a cushion 84-5

Calico 27
Canopy for bed 105-6
Care and maintenance 28-9, 73
Cartridge pleats 35
Chintz 28
Choice of fabrics 24-5
Choosing a window style 30, 32
Circular tablecloth 59-61
Classic style lampshade 110-13
Cone lampshade 91-4
Coronet for bed 105-6
Cotton wool holders 67-9
Covered coat hangers 65-7

Cover for lampshade 92-3, 110-13
Cover for tissue boxes 130-2
Covering piping cord 20
Curtain heading tapes 33
Curtains 30-6, 44-7, 70-3, 95-8, 132-4
Curtain tie-backs 98-103
Cushions 37-8, 47-9, 80-2, 84-5, 126-7, 132
Cutting on the cross 17
Cutting out curtains and blinds 36

Decorative borders 15-16
Domette 27
Double photograph frame 62-3
Down 27
Downproof cambric 27
Dressing table cover 108-10
Duvet covers 85-7

Edges 16-17
Equipment and tools 21-3
Estimating fabric requirements for curtains 35-6

Fabric-covered canisters 67-9
Fabric-covered photograph frames 61-3
Fabrics 24, 27
Feathers 37
Festoon blinds 121-3
Fillings 37-8
Firm lampshade 39-40
Fitted sheets 87-9
Flat fell seam 13
Frames for lampshades 42
French seam 12
Frilled cushions 47-9

Frilled pillowcase 90-1
Frills 16, 44, 47, 124

Gathered bed valance 54-7
Gathered frill 16
Gathered heading 33
Gathered valance 103-5
Gingham 28

Heading tapes 33-5, 72, 96
Hemming 10
Herb cushions 63-4
Herringbone stitch 8
Holland 28

Interlined curtains 95-8
Interlinings 33, 74-5, 95

Joining bias strips 17
Joining piping cord 20

Kapok 37

Lace 27
Lace bedspread 53
Lampshade fabrics 39
Lampshades 39-43, 57-8, 91-4, 110-13
Lapped seam 12
Latex foam 38
Lavender sachets 63-5
Lined curtains 70-3
Linen union 28
Lining for lampshade 112-13
Lining sateen 28
Linings 32-3, 76
Lockstitch 10
Loose covers 124-5

Maintenance 28-9
Measures 22
Measuring for curtains 35-6
Mitred corners 14-15, 54-5

Needles 21

Ottomans, loose cover 124-5
Outside tacking 11
Overcasting 8

Padded hangers 65-7
Pad for cushions 38

Pelmet buckram 27, 73-5, 100-1, 109
Pelmets 73-7, 109-10
Pencil-pleated heading 33, 70-3
Photograph frames 61-3
Pillowcases 89-91
Pillow ticking 28
Pinch-pleated heading 33, 95-8
Pins 21
Piping cord 20
Plain sheets 87
Plaited tie-back 102-3
Pleated firm lampshade 57-8
Pleated frill 16, 49
Pot pourri sachets 63-5

Quilted bedspread 51, 53

Roller blinds 77-80
Roman blinds 114-17
Round frilled cushion 48-9
Running stitch 8

Scissors 22
Seam ripper 22
Seams 12-14
Serge stitch 10
Sewing machine 23
Shaped tie-back 100-2
Shower cap 134-5
Shower curtain 132-4
Single photograph frame 61-2
Slipstitch 10
Squab cushion 26-7
Square frilled cushion 47-8
Stencilling 77-8, 94
Stiffened pelmets 73-7
Stitches 8-11
Stool cover 124
Style 26-7
Swags and tails 117-20
Synthetic wadding 27

Tablecloths 59-60
Tacking 8
Tailored bedcover 82-3
Tailor's chalk 22
Tails and swags 117-20
Techniques 15-20
Thimbles 22
Threads 21
Throw-over bedspreads 50-1, 53

Tie-backs 98-103
Ties for cushions 126-7
Tissue box cover 130-2
Tools and equipment 21-3
Touch and close fastening 73, 84, 87, 105
Towel trims 134
Tracks and fittings 32
Trimmings 42-3, 113
Trunk cover 124

Unbleached calico 27
Unlined curtains 44-7
Upholstery pins 22

Valances 53-7, 103-5
Velvet 28

Wadded edge 97-8
Wadding 27, 38, 98
Wastepaper bins 67-9